GROWING UP X

GROWING UP X

Ilyasah Shabazz

with Kim McLarin

ONE WORLD
THE BALLANTINE PUBLISHING GROUP
NEW YORK

This book is dedicated to my five sisters, *Attallah, Qubilah, Gamilah, Malikah, and Malaak*—all of whom I love deeply. Sisters, I know that life has dealt many challenges—as we have seen in Mommy and Daddy's lives as well as throughout the history of mankind—only to make us stronger, wiser, and more convicted servants like those before us. Let's rejoice that each of us six girls is a proud recipient of our beloved parents' union, and that today only the six of us together can create one link needed to preserve our parents' will for tomorrow.

I pray that this little book rekindles the joy, laughter, and innocence of yesteryear, the good old days at "234" (before we had to get out there ourselves and see all from which Mommy protected us; all for which Daddy fought for us), and that we plow forward together in our Ancestors' grace— honoring our Creator, our legacy, and our inner selves.

Eternal Love.

If I could have convinced more slaves that they were slaves, I would have freed thousands more.

—HARRIET TUBMAN

Contents

CONTENTS

Acknowledgments

First and foremost, I'd like to give praise and thanks to our Creator, God, Allah, for inner peace, continued love, and patience toward understanding the essence of life itself and its bountiful blessings. To the Ancestors that predated the Holocaust of Brown people, when Black really was Beautiful (let's say 10,000 B.C.), thank you for leaving us history (the pyramids, the Sphinx, the Nile Valley, and all the uses of natural resources, the Stars, the Sciences, Math, Architecture, Music, Fashion, Perfumes, and so much more); the fundamental principles of our African culture—Universal Spirit and Intellect. To the enslaved Ancestors, for making a majestic way out of no way, cultivating the soil of the earth for all of us today.

Mommy and Daddy, for your unconditional love and servitude . . . for living an exemplary life with faith in the Most High, of human decency, and determination; for shedding Light on our ancestors' true contributions to world history. My Big Sis, Attallah, for keeping me whole when I questioned my existence. Thank you, Sis!

Qubilah, for being in the right place at the right time. My baby sisters: Gamilah, for keeping me laughing; the twins, Malikah, for being so smart, kind, and sweet, and Malaak, for your intellect and continued talking over and over and over again.

To my mother and father's families before and after them, God bless you, including my nephews, Malcolm and Malik, and my niece, Bettih-Bahiyah. May you clearly understand your lineage, make a commitment to Justice, live life in honor of a great Legacy, carrying on the struggle of human decency in the name of Allah while enjoying without limitations a happy and productive life of your own.

My most dear and special Aunt Hilda and
Uncle Wesley Little.
Blessed are the pure in heart for they shall see God. Matthew 5:8

The Wallace Family (Thomas, Antoinette, Tommy, and Gail Wallace-Miller), words are simply not enough for when my parents in turn needed "true" love; they found peace in each of you. . . . Mr. Percy Sutton, thank you for being with us from the beginning and after the end. Sister Aisha al-Adawiya, Dr. Maya Angelou, Laura Ross Brown, Haki Madabuhti, Auntie Mary Redd, Dr. Niara Sudarkasa, thank you for your warm comfort.

My dearest sisterfriends . . . Lisa Anthony, Crystal Christmas, Ayala Donchin, Dawn Ellerby, Claudine Grier, Kathy Hill, Liz Loblack, Danielle Philogene, Kathy Rimmer, Lisa Simone Stroud, Tammy Taylor, Sybil and Adrienne Testamark—through the mountains, rivers, and valleys, we sisters are a constant. My most dear cousin Ilyasah LeAsah Little-Brown. Cousin? You are my Light! Nadia Gourzong, I could not have been blessed with a finer goddaughter. Robert, God has certainly brought us together. Thank you for sharing you. Thank you for your love, your peace, and your faith.

To my editor, Anita Diggs. When the struggle seemed to be in vain, thank you for your assurance. Thank you for your commitment. Thank you for sharing this higher vision. Thank you for understanding the need to preserve this brief portion of history. Without you, this could not have been possible. Thank you. Thank you. Thank you. Thank you. My cowriter, Miss Kim McLarin—the novelist! Truly, you are a blessing from above. Thank you for your organizational skills. Thank you for your talents. Thank you for sorting through all of this and always staying ahead of the race.

Auntie Coretta Scott King for staying in all six of our courts, offering encouragement and comfort just as our mother did, when there seemed to be no one else physically around. Jean Anderson Owensby, you know you are the true angel in this literary journey. Thank you, Precious! And to my dear friend Julie Wells Bearden and my soul sister Terrie Williams—you two of all know my heart because it is a reflection of yours! Thank you for all of you.

We come into each other's life for a specific purpose. When that purpose is fulfilled, all we can do is reminisce, learn, readjust, and then simply move on. And sometimes we're blessed to have certain angels in our lives for a lifetime. I am grateful to all of you who have touched my life so fervently. Understanding life in this manner makes it easier to enjoy those special moments yet gracefully let go in deeper peace. . . .

ACKNOWLEDGMENTS

Additional Acknowledgments

Tony Abney, Malaika Adero, Muhammad Ali, Dr. Norma Jean Anderson, Peter Bailey, Safiya Bandele, Amiri Baraka, Amy Billingsley, Kim Brown, Cousin Shahara Little-Brown, Camp Betsey Cox (Muffin, Nanette, Lemon, Candy, Liz, Lori, Mandy, Patty, Shirley, Chrissy, Beth) founders Jean "Mrs. D" Davies and Mike and Lorrie Byrom, Denise Carter, Nicholas Cherot, The Cortlandt Manor Girls Dawna, Kim, Mayma, Robin, Sean "P. Diddy" Combs, Mayor Ernest Davis, Ossie and Ruby Dee Davis, Larry and Olga Dais, DMX, Michael Eric Dyson, Noel and Wilma Fearon, Tom Feelings, Derek Ferguson, Joseph Fleming, Herman Fulton, Jackie and Jeffrey Grant, Dr. Bruce Greenstein, Dick Gregory, Robert Haggins, Alex Haley, David A. Harris, Dorothy Heights, Gil Scott Herron, Rita Howard, Karen Hunter, Jack and Jill, Inc., Westchester County Chapter, Dr. Ed O. Jackson, Janet Jackson, Norman Jewison, Magic Johnson, Cousin Debbie Little-Jones, John and Fran Keefe, Mayor Ed Koch, Yuri Kochiyama, Spike Lee, The Links, Inc., and The Greater Hudson Valley Chapter, Kevin MacRae, Nelson and Winnie Mandela, Dr. Manning Marble, Kedar Massenburg, Judge Grey Mathis, Curtis Mayfield, Dr. Henry L. McCurtis, Doug Messiah, Minyon Moore, Alanis Morrisette, MeShell Ndegocello, Gil Noble, Gordon Parks, Julio Peterson, Sidney and Juanita Poitier, Kenneth Ramseur, Charles Rangel, Merrill Roberts, Candace, Sandy, and Souls of my sisters, Yoshi Scarboro, Carl Scott, Jill Scott, Rev. Al Sharpton, Tracy Sherrod, Pamela Shine, Russell Simmons, Nina Simone, Cherron Tomlinson, Iyanla VanZant, James Walker, Mike Wallace, Dionne Warwick, Denzel Washington, Jitu Weusi, Brother Preston Wilcox, Marvin Worth, and Oprah Winfrey.

Author's Note

It is not my intention to rehash my father's life. He has told his life story in the *Autobiography of Malcom X*, which you can read for details of his incredible journey. *Growing Up X* is simply an interpretation of my life—one of six daughters of Malcolm X and Dr. Betty Shabazz.

GROWING UP X

Prologue

One of the last times I saw Mommy whole and smiling and beautiful was Mother's Day of 1997.

I took her out to dinner at the Audubon Café, along with my friend Kathy and her mother, whom I called Auntie Wilma. At the last minute, Mommy invited her friend Mary Redd to join us. We loved Auntie Redd as much as Mommy, but we had not expected her and so we were caught unprepared; we had no gift for her. As Mommy and Auntie Wilma began opening their presents, Mommy leaned over and whispered to me, "Go find some flowers for Mary Redd. I don't want her to feel left out." Kathy and I flew out the door.

When we came back with the flowers, Mommy, true to form, tried to sneak me money. She insisted, but I'm not her daughter for nothing; I told her to put her money back in her purse.

Afterward, Mommy took us to the site of the old Audubon Ballroom, which Columbia University was developing into a biotechnology research center. Mommy expressed her concerns about the promises that were not kept in making the center a real and living memorial to her husband, Malcolm X. She showed us the life-size bronze sculpture of Daddy downstairs and told us how she had wanted the artist to change the suit he was wearing because "My husband didn't wear Armani. He wore single-breasted suits. He was conservative." (The artist, Ms. Gabriel Koren, changed the suit.) Then she took us upstairs to the ballroom and showed us the beautiful mural depicting Daddy's life. She told us how she had instructed the artist, Mr. Daniel Galvez, to paint a bassinet in one area because her fourth baby, Gamilah, would feel left out if he did not. She also made sure the artist positioned the crescent and star on Daddy's ring correctly. "If you're gonna do something, do it right," she said, just the way she'd said it a million times before. "And for God's sake, follow through."

It was a wonderful evening for me, spent in the physical presence of one of the most important people in my life and the spiritual presence of the other. When it was time to part, I kissed Mommy on the cheek and gave her a big hug.

"Good night, Mommy. I love you. Happy Mother's Day."

Two weeks later, on the first day of June, I attended a play in Mount Vernon, New York, with my friend Crystal and her six-year-old daughter Nia. The play was *Endangered Species* by Judy Shepherd King and it was about how young people and their families can battle the scourge of the violence, drugs, and AIDS that is afflicting our communities.

It was a special event for me; in my capacity as director of public relations for the city of Mount Vernon, I had spent weeks courting press coverage for the event, and the turnout was great. Doug Watson of Black Entertainment Television was on hand, as were many other journalists. Overall, the event was a rousing success and I was pleased. At one point in the evening Doug pulled me aside and whispered he had just run into my mother and my nephew Malcolm at a nearby restaurant, The Bayou. "They looked like they were having a good time," Doug said. I was sure they were; Mommy liked to enjoy herself when she could. Part of me wanted to sneak out and join them, but of course I couldn't leave.

After the performance, Crystal, Nia, and I drove to Manhattan for dinner. By the time I made it back to my apartment in Mount Vernon it was nearly one o'clock in the morning. I was so weary I had barely enough energy to brush my teeth and wash my face before falling into bed. I am a hard sleeper; my mother could tell you from years of experience that trying to wake me up when I'm tired is like trying to raise a stone. When I was in high school, my poor mom would come to my room at 5:00 A.M. and beg me to get up before I missed my bus.

But early that morning something shook me from my sleep. It was a presence, a soundless voice that warned *Wake up! Your mother needs you!* I bolted straight up in bed, frightened and confused. A voice was speaking words into my answering machine, and somewhere in the kitchen my pager was beeping wildly.

Frightened, I jumped out of bed and ran to the kitchen. Along the way I noticed the light on my answering machine blinking furiously, but before I could listen to the message the telephone rang again. I picked it up. It was a stranger's voice, and she identified herself as a nurse, calling from Jacobi Hospital.

"Your mother has been in a fire," she said.

I felt as though someone had punched me, hard, right in the chest, but I couldn't fall to the floor like I wanted to. Terror was propping me up. "Is it bad?" I managed to ask.

The nurse spoke softly but did not hesitate. "Yes."

She gave me directions to the hospital. I didn't think to call anyone to go with me, either my sisters or a girlfriend. I didn't think of taking a cab, even though my hands were shaking so hard and my heart was pounding so fast I was in no real shape to drive. I didn't think of anything except getting to Mommy, and the next thing I knew I was in my car, racing toward the hospital.

How the hospital officials got my phone number I'm not sure. They didn't even know who my mother was before I arrived; when I got there, she was listed as Jane Doe. I rushed into the emergency room, disheveled and dismayed, and told the attendant I was there for my mother who had been in a fire. She took my arm and escorted me to the back.

"Try to prepare yourself," she said. "It's bad."

I was so terrified I could barely stand. By now only an emergency room curtain separated us. The nurse looked at me, but I was too frightened to even raise my hand. How could I see her this way? How could I have this be the impression of my mother I would carry with me for the rest of my life?

A doctor appeared out of nowhere, that look of practiced sympathy pasted on his face. He introduced himself, ran through some gibberish my mind refused to take in, and then reiterated those words I had been hearing all too often that night.

"I should tell you it's bad," he said. "You need to prepare for the worst."

I wanted to scream at these people who kept telling me how bad it was. Didn't they know who they were dealing with? Didn't they know who she was? My mother had been through the worst possible pain in her life and emerged unbroken, carrying her six daughters and so much of the world on her back.

What could possibly be so bad that Mommy couldn't handle it? All my life, my mother had been the tree against which I and my sisters and so many other people had leaned. She was the one whose personal motto, despite all the pain she had suffered in life, was "Find the good and praise it."

How in the world could a woman like that possibly fall?

Aftermath

I *was there that day.* We all were, all except baby Gamilah who, in the last-minute rush to go hear Daddy speak, got left behind with friends because her little snowsuit was too damp to wear out into the cold. But the rest of us were there, sitting stage right on a curved and cushioned bench: Mommy, Attallah, Qubilah, myself. Even the twins, Malikah and Malaak, were present to bear witness, carried not in Mommy's arms but inside her womb, deep beneath her heart.

It was February 21, 1965. My father, El-Hajj Malik El-Shabazz—Malcolm X—telephoned my mother at the Wallace home that morning with a surprising request. He wanted Mommy to bring us girls and come to the Audubon Ballroom in Harlem to hear him speak. My mother was elated; just the day before he had warned her not to come, saying it was too dangerous.

We were staying with the Wallace family because eight days before our house in Elmhurst, Queens, had been firebombed. It was early Sunday morning and cold outside. Mommy and Daddy were asleep in their bedroom, Attallah, Qubilah, and I were in our room, and Gamilah was in the nursery when a blast awakened us all. Barking orders and grabbing terrified children, my father got us all up and out the back door into the yard. It took the fire department an hour to extinguish the flames. Mommy telephoned the Wallaces, saying, "The house is on fire." The Wallaces put their twelve-year-old daughter Gail—our baby-sitter and play "big sister"—in the car and drove to our house. Gail told me she remembers walking into the house and being almost overwhelmed by the smell of smoke.

"Everyone was in the kitchen," Gail said, "and to get to the kitchen you had to walk through the foyer, the living room, a long hallway, and your room, the room you girls slept in. That room was a mess, burned and wet and scattered, because that's where the bomb had been thrown. I saw all these people standing in the kitchen. I remember crawling through men and women, Muslim men, to get to your mother. She was sitting at the kitchen table talking and when she saw me she said, 'Oh, dear heart, they're trying to burn me out of my house.' She was happy to see me because she knew once I was there I would take over the girls enough so she could get the situation under control. She had a little grin on her face but it wasn't one of pleasure."

The Wallace family—Antoinette, her husband Thomas, who is Ruby Dee's brother and was known then as Thomas 57X, and their four children—took us in that night. My father made sure we were settled at the Wallace home, then checked into the Theresa Hotel (although the night before the assassination he stayed at the New York Hilton). He knew he was a walking target and he didn't want anyone else to get hit. He told Mommy he wanted to take the trouble away from us.

Four days later, the Nation of Islam went to court to evict us from our home.

In the aftermath of the fire, my father never stopped working. Friends like Ossie Davis begged him to flee. His brother Wilfred advised him to "hush and forget this whole thing" and go to Africa until things cooled down. There were any number of African nations whose leaders would have been happy to offer him refuge, but Daddy refused to even discuss the idea. He was not about to run. He took what security precautions he could, but through it all he kept working, flying to Detroit to speak at an event in honor of Charles Howard, a renowned journalist who covered the African liberation movement for *Muhammad Speaks* and other black newspapers, then turning around and flying back home to New York for another flurry of speaking engagements and interviews. In between all this activity, he worked hard to find a new home for all of us.

He knew the end was coming soon.

Percy Sutton tells a story of sitting in the backseat of a car with Daddy and two armed guards around this time. Mr. Sutton asked my father if it bothered him being surrounded by people with guns.

My father said to him, "Have I told you the story of Omar the slave? Omar said to his master, 'Give me your fastest horse, I'm going to escape the Face of Death.' It being a slave belief that if you rode by day and got through the day with the swiftness of the horse, you were safe by night. There were seven paths down which Omar could go. He started down the center path, pulled the horse back. Started to the left, and pulled back again. Only a short distance down the third path stood the Face of Death. Death said to Omar, 'For three days I've waited at this spot for you to come. Why has it taken you so long?' " And then Minister Malcolm said, "So you see, counselor, you can twist, you can turn, but there's destiny."

Meanwhile we stayed with the Wallaces and waited for Daddy. The NYPD sat outside the Wallace home and followed us everywhere. They even followed the Wallace children to school, until Gail Wallace and her siblings gave them the slip by sneaking out the back window. They said they were there to help but no one believed it. What they were really doing was shadowing my father, casing him and his movements, preparing for February 21.

On February 20 Daddy came by the Wallace house to check on us. As he was leaving, Brother Thomas asked what he could do to help. Our exhausted-looking father shook his head. "It's something unseen all around me," he told Brother Thomas. Then he climbed into his car and drove away.

"A funny feeling came over me hearing that," Mrs. Wallace told me years later. "I felt like I was seeing this man for the last time."

So when Daddy called that morning of February 21 and asked us to come hear him speak, Mommy was happy. She loved Daddy and missed him and wanted to be present for support. She hurried about, dressing herself and us, then Brother Thomas drove us into Manhattan and up to Harlem to the Audubon. We arrived just after noon.

After we left the telephone rang and Mrs. Wallace answered it.

It was Wallace Muhammad, son of Elijah Muhammad. Elijah Muhammad was the spiritual leader of the Nation of Islam, the man my father had once credited with saving his life and the man whose followers my father now suspected were among those who wanted to take it. Wallace Muhammad was agitated. He said he'd been trying to reach my father for days. He wanted to warn him, to tell him they were going to kill him soon. He did not say who "they" were.

Brother Thomas dropped us off at the front door and went to park the car. I cannot begin to imagine my mother's feelings as she ushered us into that ballroom to hear her husband speak. My mother loved my father deeply, and she admired his commitment to changing the lives of black people in America and throughout the world. But she also knew the toll that work had taken on him. She knew how draining was the constant traveling, how wearing were the harassment by the FBI and the intimidation by the members of the Nation of Islam. She knew how deeply pained he was by the attack on the house where his wife and daughters lay asleep. She knew how tired he was, and she knew that as much as she wanted to make it all better, she couldn't. No one could.

I imagine my mother walked into that ballroom full of joy, pride, anxiety, love, and not a little fear.

And she walked out shattered in a way that could never, ever be repaired.

I write all this as though I remember, which I do not, Allah be praised. I was two years old, going on three, and though I surely felt confusion and fear at the time, I have no memory of any of it. From these experiences I carry only a dislike of endings, a lingering uneasiness with good-byes. My oldest sister, Attallah, was six years old when my father was assassinated; Qubilah was four. How much, exactly, they remember is something we never discussed while growing up. Somehow Mommy kept us so busy and fulfilled we never talked about it, or maybe it was just too hard. It wasn't until recently, just a few years ago, that I finally asked Qubilah if she remembered that day. I was in graduate school working on a paper and she was visiting me. We began discussing the condition of African people throughout the world, and from there the conversation turned to Daddy and his work.

Yes, she said. She remembered him and she remembered that day in all its confusion and terror. She remembered noise and screaming and confusion and Daddy not coming home.

I didn't push her on her memories. Really, what more was there to say?

It was a fairly mild February afternoon. Outside the Audubon, children played on the street while Christian men and women strolled home from Sunday church services. My mother took us girls and went inside the auditorium, which was quickly filling up. More than four hundred people, many of them non-Muslim, had come to hear Malcolm X speak. He had promised earlier to present the charter of his newly formed Organization of Afro-American Unity on that day, but the drafting committee had fallen behind, the charter was unfinished, and he was upset. My father did not like to break his word.

We sat right up front in a reserved booth near the stage where we could see our father clearly and be sure he saw us. We settled in; my mother took off our snowsuits. My father was backstage, preparing to speak. The ballroom grew full. Time passed. The program was late getting started because they were waiting for two invited guests, the Reverend Dr. Milton Galamison, a civil rights activist, and Ralph Cooper, a popular disk jockey. After awhile my father's assistant, Benjamin X, took the stage. He spoke for about twenty minutes. He talked about a ship crossing the ocean, about the storms and trade winds and doldrums and other delays that might keep even a well-captained ship from reaching its destination on time, alluding to the delayed charter. Then he introduced Daddy.

My father walked onto the stage to applause and gave the familiar greeting. "As-salaam alaikum, brothers and sisters." (May peace be unto you.)

"Wa-alaikum salaam," the audience responded. (May peace be unto you, too.)

Just then, a few rows back from the front, a disturbance occurred. Some kind of scuffle, a man's voice saying, angrily, "Get your hand out of my pocket!" Everyone in the audience turned to look.

My father raised his hands, trying to calm the situation. "Hold it! Hold it! Don't get excited," my father said. "Let's cool it, brothers—"

Or something like that. Those words come via Alex Haley, who "wrote" my father's autobiography. Other witnesses remember different words from Malcolm X, but whatever his words, his intent was clear: to calm the situation, to diffuse what he thought was tension among his own. My mother, in her testimony before the grand jury investigating my father's death, recalled her husband's last words as these: "Everything's all right." Such soothing words.

Using the distraction as cover, three men in the front row stood up and began firing. People screamed, dove for the ground, rushed the exits. My mother pushed us to the floor, shoved us beneath the booth and threw her body over ours, trying both to protect our lives and our innocence. I believe she knew what was happening; some already-shattered part of her knew and didn't want us to see. We were only babies. Bad enough that we had to hear the thunderous shots, the terrified screams, the chaos and crashing of chairs.

Sixteen bullets tore through my father's body, striking him in his chest, near his navel, in his thigh, knee, ankle, right hand and forearm, and left biceps. He fell backward over the chairs behind him and tumbled to the floor. In the bedlam that followed people scattered in all different directions, including toward my father onstage. They ripped open his shirt and tried to staunch the bleeding. At least two people tried to give him mouth-to-mouth resuscitation: Yuri Kochiyama, the Asian American activist, and my mother, a nurse. Someone else rushed to Columbia-Presbyterian Hospital's Vanderbilt Clinic, which was only ten blocks away, and brought back a stretcher, and they raced him to the hospital that way. Mommy went, too. A photographer got a picture of him being carried on that stretcher, head thrown back, mouth open, eyes closed.

(When I was young, that photograph was deeply disturbing and painful to me. Yet some part of me had to see it, to see his eyes, his mouth, his teeth, his chest, his arms, everything. I always wondered how he was feeling. Did it hurt? Was he scared? What was he thinking? I could never look at that photograph without half-covering my eyes, but I wanted to look at it. I wanted to see him and whatever was happening to him. It is easier for me now, as an adult, to see that photograph. Now I know that whatever the appearance of his body at that moment, his soul was at peace.)

He was declared deceased at 3:30 P.M., but he probably passed away before that.

All that I know about that terrible, terrible day I have learned from the *Autobiography*, from other written sources, and from the painful recollections of friends, including the Wallaces. My mother herself never spoke to us about what happened on February 21, 1965. My mother would not revisit that moment, ever. She could not.

We girls were brought back to the house by someone, probably Brother Thomas. Our mother wasn't with us. Our father wasn't with us. We were terrified. The living room in the Wallace house was dark. The adults were wet-eyed and shaking. We were all sobbing, though probably only Attallah and Qubilah really understood the reason for our tears. Qubilah looked up at Gail Wallace and asked, "Is Daddy dead?"

Gail was only twelve, but we looked up to her. She was our baby-sitter and our friend; she took care of us and so naturally we expected her to have the answers. "I didn't know what to say," she told me many years later. "I was a little girl, too."

17

———

My mother did not take us to the funeral, held on February 27, 1965, at the Faith Temple, Church of God in Christ, at 147th Street and Amsterdam Avenue. We did not see the more than seventeen hundred people packed into the church nor the six thousand plus mourners waiting outside in the bitter cold. We did not hear the telegrams of condolences from every major civil rights organization and dozens of Middle Eastern dignitaries, from Dr. Martin Luther King Jr., the ambassador from Lagos, the president of the Republic of Ghana. We did not see our father's body wrapped in the delicate white winding cloth of Muslim burials.

We did not hear Ossie Davis deliver his stirring eulogy: "Many will ask what Harlem finds to honor in this stormy, controversial, and bold young captain—and we will smile. . . . They will say that he is of hate—a fanatic, a racist—who can only bring evil to the cause for which you struggle.

"And we will answer and say unto them: Did you ever talk to Brother Malcolm? Did you ever touch him or have him smile at you? Did you ever really listen to him? Did he ever do a mean thing? Was he ever himself associated with violence or any public disturbance? For if you did you would know him. And if you knew him you would know why we must honor him: Malcolm was our manhood, our living black manhood. This was his meaning to his people. And in honoring him, we honor the best in ourselves. . . . And we will know him then for what he was and is—a Prince, our own black shining Prince!—who didn't hesitate to die because he loved us so."

We didn't see Mommy bend to kiss the glass over Daddy's coffin, then burst into tears.

I don't remember what we did the rest of that day. Probably we stayed at home with Mrs. Wallace and her daughters and did whatever little girls do when some terrible event beyond their imagining has occurred and the grieving adults around them don't know how to begin to explain. Played with dolls. Colored with crayons. Ate some snacks.

Wondered when Mommy and Daddy would be home.

CHAPTER TWO

Alone

A few years ago I traveled to Chicago to accept an award in honor of my father. At a party afterward I met this white guy. For the sake of this story, let's call him Ed.

We were standing side by side in the VIP section of the club when Ed turned to me and said something like, "That girl should not be wearing those pants unless she means to send the kind of signal she's sending." I was so startled I laughed—first, because I actually thought the pants were pretty nice, and second, because it was such a surprising thing for a man to have an opinion about, at least one he would share with a woman he did not know. Ed must have taken my laughter as a sign of encouragement, because the next thing I knew he was giving me a running commentary about all the white women in the room and how he could tell who was "fast" just by the pants they were wearing. From there we moved on to women versus men, Chicago versus New York, and a host of other topics. It was a fun conversation and I was having a good time, intrigued by how much a man's point of view differed from a woman's.

After a few more minutes of conversation, Ed smiled. "You know, you're a very beautiful woman," he said.

"Thanks."

"Not only beautiful, but sexy." Ed leaned in. "And very cool. That's nice. You don't seem to have any hang-ups. That's unusual."

I smiled back at Ed, trying to walk that line between being nice and encouraging what was obviously turning into a pass. He seemed like a decent and even innocent guy, but I was not interested. Still, I thought I knew what he was talking about. I've always been teased by my family about my openness, my willingness to walk right up to strangers and talk to them as if they were long-lost friends. "Hang-ups? Like what?"

"You know," Ed said. "Black hang-ups. Racial hang-ups. You're so self-assured, and so open. That's nice. You don't seem to be carrying a chip on your shoulder."

It turned out that one of Ed's best friends was African American, a man he had roomed with in college and cared about in a brotherly way. But no matter how close the two men were, how many footballs they tossed or six-packs they shared, Ed felt that something always kept them from becoming really good friends. Something stood between them; Ed believed it was his friend's deep and unreasonable distrust of white people.

"He's not open like you are," Ed said. "He has hang-ups, big time."

"Really?"

"Oh, yeah," Ed assured me. "In fact, a lot of black guys I know are like that. I don't understand it."

The party was warming up and I could have just shrugged and walked away. But Ed looked so genuinely perplexed, and a little sad, something in me wanted to explain. But where to begin?

We talked for a while and I tried to explain why the brothers might feel the way Ed described. I steered the conversation to Malcolm X, discussing his contributions and his legacy and the impact Malcolm X had and continues to have to this day on African Americans like his friend. I didn't reveal my relationship; I like to hear what people think about my father without them knowing he's my father. The results are sometimes exhilarating, sometimes absolutely ridiculous, but always informative.

In this case, Ed had the usual narrow, fragmented, and, in some ways, completely false understanding of Malcolm X and his contribution to this country and the world. Ed suggested Malcolm X was a fire-breathing radical who more than distrusted white people—he hated and despised them.

"Are you kidding? Malcolm X was ten times worse than my friend!" Ed laughed. "Didn't he call us all blue-eyed devils? Didn't he want nothing to do with us?"

"So you don't think Malcolm X would have a daughter like me?" I asked.

Ed shook his head hard. "No way!" he said. "No way."

I like to tell that story because it says so much—not only about how deeply and sadly Malcolm X is misunderstood in America today, but also about how that misunderstanding often casts its shadow upon my sisters and myself.

Being the daughter of Malcolm X and Dr. Betty Shabazz is a gift for which I am forever grateful. Malcolm X was a man absolutely committed to changing the way people of African descent viewed themselves, one another, and their place in world history. He attempted to destroy the psychological scars and racial barriers that kept a people from reaching its full potential. He gave African Americans one of the greatest gifts possible, the gift of self-respect. He is my hero and my mother is my heroine. I wouldn't change that for anything in this world.

Yet growing up as the child of two such astonishingly strong and determined people wasn't always easy. When people hear the name Malcolm X they tend to have a strong reaction, either quite positive or very negative, like Ed. Each reaction carries its own weight.

Mommy did a remarkable job of shielding my sisters and me from all that when we were children, but she could not shield us forever. In my adolescence and early adulthood, the expectations of those who knew and admired my father and mother became a heavy burden. How could I possibly be as forthright or as smart or as disciplined as my father? How could I be as strong or determined as my mother? Why were people surprised—and sometimes disappointed—when they learned how normal my childhood was, how mainstream and privileged and integrated and utterly American?

I rarely tell people whose daughter I am when meeting them for the first time. But in the case of Ed of Chicago, I decided to break my rule. For some reason, it seemed important to make a point.

"Ed," I said, "Malcolm X is my father."

Had his mouth dropped open any wider Ed would have been able to swallow the entire party buffet without pausing to chew.

From my earliest days I have only fragments of memory: a blue-and-white rocking chair, pink tights I didn't want to wear to preschool, the sound of my sisters laughing at bedtime.

I remember one day waking up and finding no one home but the housekeeper. I don't know how old I was then, two, maybe three, but old enough to wonder where my mother was, where my sisters had gone. I toddle to the dining room window and look out into the street, searching. I'm so big for my age anyone looking back at me must wonder why a five-year-old is running around in baby clothes with a bonnet on her head. I put my hands on the blinds and pull them apart and put my face there, too, searching for Mommy and my sisters. I feel scared and very alone.

My clearest early memory is of Mommy. I remember being three or four years old and looking up at her and thinking how beautiful she is. No doubt all young children cast their mothers in the role of fairy princess, and I was just the same. Mommy was a striking woman. She had clear brown Egyptian eyes and a stately Masai carriage. My father, who was so fair he had once been nicknamed Red, loved my mother's smooth, mahogany skin. He called her his Apple Brown Betty and Brown Sugar.

I remember one day looking at Mommy and thinking, "Wow!" She was wearing sailor pants, cut full and flowing at the hem, decorated with heavy black buttons and made of a thick and luxurious material. She had on slender, black patent leather boots with square toes and a long black coat that danced around her legs when she moved. Her hair was swept up off her face, showing off her beautiful eyes and her incredible cheekbones. She was going into the cleaners, leaving us in the car with the baby-sitter while she did what she had to do. Watching her cross the street I felt my breath catch in my throat. She looked so lovely and so majestic that I wanted to clap my hands and laugh. People checked her out as she passed; she was such a heart-stopper I almost expected them to hail her as she walked, to toss rose petals beneath those boots. It was clear to me and it was clear to the throngs along the avenue: Mommy was an African queen.

"I didn't sleep for three months after my husband's death, because every time I would try to sleep, I would see him falling."
—MOMMY IN AN *EBONY* MAGAZINE INTERVIEW, 1968

God only knows how Mommy made it through those first weeks and months following my father's death. My father was not only her husband, he was the great love of her life. To have witnessed his violent death must have seemed more than she could bear.

To make matters worse, Mommy was now homeless; the fire-bombing and the Nation of Islam's eviction had taken care of that. She had little money; my father had always believed the Nation would take care of his family should the need arise, and so he never sought to enrich himself, only the organization. He didn't even have life insurance because by the time he knew he needed it, no insurance company would touch him.

Nor was Mommy soothed by an outpouring of public support, in the way Jacqueline Kennedy and Coretta Scott King were when their husbands fell to assassins. The major press considered my father a fire-breathing, white-hating maniac who'd been cut down by members of his own strange and subversive cult. Some considered his death poetic justice. The *New York Times* editorialized him as "a twisted man" who turned "true gifts to evil purpose." Carl

Rowan, then director of the United States Information Agency and later a columnist for the *Washington Post*, dismissed my father as an "ex-convict, ex–dope peddler who became a racial fanatic."

Mr. Rowan was not the only prominent African American who kept his distance. The same middle-class, integration-minded blacks who had disavowed Malcolm X in life wanted nothing to do with his widow. I have been told by people who were there that bells of alarm went off in certain Mount Vernon circles when word got out that Mommy had purchased a house in that enclave of upwardly mobile, aspiring African American professionals. *Whose widow? Living here? We don't want any trouble.* Guess who's coming to the neighborhood.

And, of course, the people my father had counted on to care for his family should anything ever happen to him—the Nation of Islam—were the very ones who conspired with government agencies to assassinate him. We had no contact with them or they with us. Even after all my father did for the Nation, we were basically left to fend for ourselves.

(We did, however, continue to root for one particular member of the Nation—Muhammad Ali. My father had known Ali when he was a rising young boxer known as Cassius Clay, before he became heavyweight champion of the world. In fact, my whole family visited Ali at his camp in Miami when he was training to fight Sonny Liston for the championship. My father wrote he would be forever grateful to Ali for the invitation. It was the first real vacation Daddy and Mommy had had together because my father was always so busy working for the cause. It also came at a painful time, just as the depth of my father's estrangement from Elijah Muhammad was becoming clear. Daddy had just been silenced by Mr. Muhammad for commenting on the assassination of John F. Kennedy, and "death-talk" against him was filling the air for the first time. My father was reeling, not from fear for his life but from the agony of betrayal. He had loved and admired Mr. Muhammad so deeply. "My head felt like it was bleeding inside," he wrote in the *Autobiography*. "I felt like my brain was damaged."

Meanwhile, in Miami, the odds were against Ali. Most people, including Nation of Islam officials in Chicago, gave him little or no chance of winning the fight. But Ali was a student of my father's; they shared a special bond. On the night of the fight my father told him, "Do you think Allah has brought about all this intending for you to leave the ring as anything but the champion?" Together they prayed to Allah before the fight.

The rest is history. Ali won, told the world he was a Muslim, and announced his new name. He and my father parted friends that day, but later on, after the split, Ali refused to talk to Daddy.

In his mind Ali was being a faithful Muslim and a dutiful son. Elijah Muhammad had forbidden all members of the Nation to associate with my father and Ali obeyed, though surely it broke his heart. I know Daddy understood and even admired Ali's sense of commitment and loyalty. Still, it hurt him to lose his friend, a man he thought of as a younger brother. Daddy loved Ali and so did Mommy. So did we all.

So whenever Ali was fighting, we girls and Mommy watched and cheered and screamed and rooted him on. Watching Ali dance across the ring was not like watching anyone else; we felt as though a member of our family was up there beneath the lights, getting his face smashed. Or smashing someone else's face. It was scary and painful and, most of all, exhilarating when that final bell rang and he lifted his gloved fist into the air. Between rounds, my sisters and I would run to the study where the Qur'an sat elevated on a special wooden holder and say a few quick prayers for his success.

Ali would, in time, come to regret the stand he took against Daddy. He would tell me himself how much he loved Malcolm X.

But my mother did have her supporters; among the most steadfast of them was Percy Sutton, who had become my father's attorney about six years before his assassination. Mr. Sutton, along with his brother and another attorney, helped my mother raise the money to buy our new house. Actors Ruby Dee and Ossie Davis gave tremendous support, both financial and emotional. The Wallace family generously housed us for about a month after my father's assassination. After that, we moved, for a brief time, to a hotel, then to the home of Sidney Poitier and his wife at the time, Juanita Poitier. They were friends of the family, activists, and supporters of the movement, and they must have wanted to help my mother in whatever way they could.

I remember the Poitier house; it was big, absolutely huge. The outside property was lush and beautifully landscaped; it seemed like a magic garden to me. I would wander through the maze of shrubs and flowers, feeling enchanted and free. But one time I got lost. I was petrified because it seemed like everything engulfed me and I couldn't find my way out. It must have been Easter, because we were having an Easter egg hunt. I remember because, when they found me, I was choking. I'd found an egg and was busy chomping through the shell. Why, I don't know. It must have looked like candy to me, magical candy. I must have thought I could stuff the whole colorful egg in my mouth and have it dissolve on my tongue like the sweetest cotton candy.

There were other friends, too: Maya Angelou, the novelist John Oliver Killens. And much, much later, when we girls were grown, my mother became close to other famous widows of the revolution: Myrlie Evers-Williams and Coretta Scott King. That fact may come as a surprise to people who like to cast my father and Martin Luther King Jr. as the black hat and white hat of the civil rights movement and, therefore, diehard enemies.

It's true they had their differences. It's true my father, especially during his early days with the Nation of Islam, disagreed with Dr. King's philosophy of nonviolent resistance. My father did not advocate violence, but he believed completely in the right of African Americans to defend themselves against violence and hostility just like anyone else. It's true my father went to Selma during Dr. King's sojourn in that city and said it was ridiculous for African American men to turn the other cheek when their women and children were being attacked by dogs and injured by fire hoses. It's true he called the March on Washington "The Farce in Washington" after whites became deeply involved in the planning of it, even to the point of censoring speeches and signs they viewed as too militant. It's true he scoffed at Dr. King's speech, saying, "Even he says it's a dream." That was Malcolm X.

While my father may have disagreed with Dr. King, he respected him. He knew they were both fighting the same fight, both completely and utterly dedicated to improving the political and social welfare of their people. Then, too, my father was a shrewd man, capable of operating on several levels at the same time. In Selma, after belittling Dr. King's nonviolent boycott for the newspapers, my father pulled Mrs. King aside.

"I want Dr. King to know that I didn't come to Selma to make his job difficult," he said. "I really did come thinking I could make it easier. If the white people realize what the alternative is, perhaps they will be more willing to hear Dr. King."

Two months before his death, my father told a group of Islamic students in Manchester, England, that he would say nothing against Dr. King. "At one time the whites in the United States called him a racialist, an extremist, and a Communist. Then the Black Muslims came along and the whites thanked the Lord for Martin Luther King."

It is vitally important to me that African Americans understand the special bond between the Shabazz and King families, because it is vitally important that we understand it's not a matter of Malcolm versus Martin. We do not have to fall into that trap and we do not have to choose. Americans aren't asked to choose between George Washington and Thomas Jefferson—both sacrificed for their country, and both are remembered for that sacrifice. Likewise, African Americans do not have to choose between Martin Luther King and Malcolm X. Both were great men who did not hesitate to die because they loved us so.

What's interesting, too, is that while the popular refrain is that Daddy was changing his views at the time of his death, moving closer to the ideals that Martin preached, no one ever mentions that when Martin Luther King was struck down he was shifting *his* beliefs closer to the ideals my father preached. King was coming to see the plight of African Americans not only as an isolated civil rights issue but as one part of an international struggle for human rights. That is a conclusion to which Malcolm X had come many years prior.

Mommy and Mrs. King understood that their husbands were great men aiming for the same goal. They eventually became close friends, as did Mommy and Myrlie Evers-Williams, the widow of Medgar Evers. They were known as "The Three Ms," the widows of three proud and dedicated African American soldiers. Our families remain close to this day. Not a holiday passes that I don't get a package from Auntie Coretta.

There were many people who helped my mother through that horrible time. She told her friend the Reverend Willie Barrow, "They came to my rescue and worked with me and worked with me and worked with me and worked with me!" I thank God for them. But I know, too, that in those early days, those days and weeks after my father was slain, no amount of friendship or support could ease the loss. My mother was a young African American woman with six babies to care for in a nation whose climate was anger and chaos and fear. Surely she felt terrified and alone.

It was somewhere in here that Mommy made her hajj, or pilgrimage to Mecca. The hajj is a journey every Muslim makes at least once in his or her lifetime if he or she is able. It is a religious obligation, a duty dictated by the Holy Qur'an. It is also a privilege and a joy.

My father had made his hajj in 1964, after his break with the Nation of Islam, after the death warrant had been issued against his life. He came home from Mecca refreshed and renewed, with a new name—El-Hajj Malik El-Shabazz—and, more important, a new understanding of orthodox Islam. He returned with a new sense of himself and his ministry, and an evolved attitude toward

America's racial problems. In a letter to my mother he wrote, "Never have I witnessed such sincere hospitality and the overwhelming spirit of true brotherhood as is practiced by people of all colors and races here in this Ancient Holy Land, the home of Abraham, Muhammad and all the other prophets of the Holy Scriptures."

My father had been planning a second trip to Mecca at the time of his murder. The people who were to accompany him asked my mother to take his place. They were offering her a trip to a place where she could immerse herself in contemplation and prayer, a place where she could be closer to the ancestors, closer to her husband, closer to God. She was a grieving new widow, the mother and sole support of four young girls, and pregnant with twins. To save her soul and her sanity, she said yes.

Later, Mommy said of her hajj, "It made me think of all the people in the world who loved me and were for me, who prayed that I would get my life back together. I stopped focusing on the people who were trying to tear me and my family apart."

One of the most important parts of the hajj experience, and the ritual that was nearest and dearest to my mother's heart, is the reenactment of the trek of Hajar, or Hagar as she is called in the Christian record. Hajar was the slave of Abraham's wife, Sarah. Abraham and Sarah were very old and childless when Abraham had a son by Hajar and named him Ishmael. But then God blessed Sarah and she had a son in her old age and named him Isaac. One day Sarah saw Isaac playing with Ishmael and said to her husband, "Cast out this slave woman with her son, for the son of this slave woman shall not inherit along with my son Isaac." So Abraham rose early one morning and took bread and water and gave it to Hajar and sent her away into the lonely desert.

When the last of their water was gone, Hajar wandered the earth in search of water for her child. In her crisis she called out to Allah. And Allah saved both her and her son. Later, Ishmael, along with Abraham, built the Kaaba, the shrine in the center of the Great Mosque in Mecca, Saudi Arabia. For followers of Islam, the Kaaba is the most sacred place on earth.

And so all pilgrims to Mecca remember Hajar's journey by running, full of sorrow and loss, between the hills of Safa and Marwa. For Mommy, just the mention of Hajar's name was enough to reduce her to tears. She had a profound affinity for her spirit and the significance of her story. Like Hajar, my mother was cast out, banished from American society in the 1960s and left to care for her children on her own without the love and support of her husband. Like Hajar, my mother trekked from one mountain of issues to another, searching for strength and relief, calling out to Allah for guidance and help. And like Hajar, my mother was greatly blessed because of the strength of her faith and the perseverance of her conviction.

While in Mecca, Mommy traveled with the traditional escort, a woman who not only looked after her physical well-being but her emotional and spiritual needs as well. It couldn't have been an easy job. The hajj is an intense spiritual journey and an arduous physical one. My mother came from a solidly middle-class background and she was not accustomed to physical hardship. Plus, she had just lost her husband to assassins and she was pregnant with twins. She wasn't pleased with the water, the crowds, the uncushioned furniture, or the seating arrangements, which involved carpets tossed onto the sand. She wasn't pleased that a man who saw her faint against a wall as she walked around in the intense heat simply walked past her without offering to help. (She understood that from the man's perspective a woman was not supposed to be walking around alone with her head uncovered, but she needed help!) She was exhausted and struggling, pregnant and unbalanced, and so she got frustrated and complained. "Why didn't that man help me? Why do we have to sit in this tent on the ground? Why can't we have a little comfort here?"

Looking back on it years later, she felt bad about her behavior. But I can't imagine anyone who knew what she had been through—and what she still had to face—held it against her.

When she returned from Mecca, Mommy, with Mr. Sutton's help, found a house for us in Mount Vernon, a city in Westchester County less than a thirty-minute train ride from New York City. Part of the down payment came from the royalties from my father's autobiography. Sidney Poiter, Ruby Dee, and others also helped out, holding fund-raising parties in our family's honor. My mother also helped make ends meet by working as a nurse when she could. But with six young daughters to raise, meager savings, and no life insurance payout, she struggled financially. My father had $600 to his name the day he was assassinated.

We lived on a tree-lined street in what is called Mount Vernon Heights, in a house that once belonged to Bella Abzug. The house was a lovely brick colonial. It sat up high on a hill; you had to climb two sets of steps to reach the front door. The landscaping emphasized graceful shrubs and ivy and a few flowers and an impeccably manicured lawn. I know it was manicured because we had to help manicure it every Saturday; my mother had the three oldest of us get out there and pick weeds. It was not an activity I enjoyed, and I didn't understand why we had to do it since we had a gardener. Now I realize Mommy was probably trying to keep our heads on straight. She worked hard to give us every advantage a child could have in this country—private schools, language lessons, summer camp—but she didn't want us growing up thinking we were too good to get down in the dirt and pull weeds.

I loved our neighborhood. Even though we lived on the corner of East 5th Street and Cedar Avenue, it was not like a regular intersection; Cedar Avenue dead-ended into the woods. This cut way down on traffic through the area and our mother felt comfortable letting us play in the cul-de-sac. I can remember hundreds of games of tag, kickball, Mother May I, red light–green light, hot peas and butter, and other childhood games.

When you walked in our front door, the first thing you saw in the foyer was a wall-sized mirror on the left and an olive green wall-to-wall leather bench on the right. Above the bench hung an ebony-framed painting of Cinque, the brave African who in 1839 led a revolt of captured slaves aboard the ship *Amistad* and later won his freedom before the U.S. Supreme Court. I loved to look at this painting and imagine myself standing proudly beside that king, which is probably just what Mommy intended. She filled our house with beautiful art by and about people of the African diaspora. Another one of my favorite pieces in the library was an ebony statue my mother got in Haiti. It was a six-foot-tall ebony carving of a woman with a fruit basket on her head and her child walking by her side.

Next to the painting of Cinque hung framed examples of our own artwork: a thought-provoking selection of neon triangles painted by me, a provocative handprint transformed into a turkey by Malaak, and other artistic creations by the rest of my sisters.

Our house was decorated tastefully and traditionally with a seventies palette. Olive green carpeting. White walls. A long blue-and-gold sofa in the living room, L-shaped and very comfortable. Behind the couch was a picture window that spanned two walls, and the drapes floating down to the floor were white. The lamps standing guard at the windows had those hanging crystals; my sisters and I used to hold them up to our ears and pretend they were earrings.

Above the piano hung a huge oil painting of my father. It was a vivid painting, done in shades of fiery red, yellow, orange, and brown, and showed him in four poses, including the famous one with his chin propped up by a hand wearing his crescent and star ring. The biggest was of him looking very serious and pointing his finger up and outward. I love that painting.

In 1969, Mommy told *Ebony* magazine it took her two years before she could hang a photograph of my father in the house—that's how painful his death was to her. But I can recall reminders of him everywhere: photographs in nearly every room, his briefcase and suits in my mother's closet, his hat way up high on a shelf in the breakfast nook, books about him in the library, especially the *Autobiography*.

The *Autobiography* was a special presence in our house. Long before my younger sisters and I had any adult comprehension of the book, we played with it. We'd read parts aloud, make up little skits about our father and his family. Sometimes we would flip to the pages with the pictures and I'd smile and say, "There's Daddy." Or I would turn to certain pages and point and say, "There's the man who was mean to Daddy." I didn't really know what I was talking about. It wasn't until years later that I realized it wasn't "the man who was mean to Daddy" but Daddy himself, in a prison photograph, but since my audience was usually my three younger sisters, I was rarely challenged on facts.

I'm not sure how much I really remember of my father. My mother and Attallah shared so many stories with us that I honestly don't know if I remember him or if the memories I have exist only because they kept him so alive.

They both spoke about him as if he had just gone out for a newspaper. Mommy talked about him when we were at dinner. She always called him "my husband." *My husband this,* and *my husband that.* Or, *Your father.* Or, *Daddy.* She told me how he would call me with authority, calling "Ilyasah!" and how I would jump! He was the only person I reacted to with such complete obedience. If my mother called me I would continue doing whatever it was I was doing, but with my father it was, "Yes sir."

I have a memory in which I used to come downstairs in our house and open the venetian blinds to look for my father. When I heard him coming, I'd go running for the door, and he'd open it and swing me up, up, up, high into the air for a big hug, then catch me under his arm like a big sack of potatoes and together we'd take the oatmeal cookies Mommy used to make and go watch the evening news.

I'm a cookie fanatic to this day, and I sleep with the news on all night long. But I'm not sure if that's a real memory. Do people really remember as toddlers? Or do they, at the age of sixteen or twenty-five or thirty, simply want to?

She kept him so alive for us.

Mommy did a heroic job of attending not only to our physical and material needs, but to our psychological ones as well. She worked for us and prayed for us. She fought for us and thought for us and sometimes spoke for us. She buffered us from life and pain as completely and as long as she could, and that was a long, long time in my case. She spoiled us, really, but she did so out of love and the desire to compensate for all that we had lost. And compensate she did, so utterly that I scarcely realized my family was incomplete. Not until I was a teenager and spent time with a friend's father did I even begin to really feel my father's absence. And not until I was a young woman and heard people talking about "single-parent households" did I realize I had, in fact, been raised in one. As a child it never occurred to me that I was part of a social phenomenon. I never felt deprived or abandoned, I never felt insufficiency or emptiness or despair or any of the things experts say children in single-parent households are supposed to feel. As far as I was concerned I had a mother and a father and a family, just like everybody. Never in my childhood did I consciously feel fatherless.

CHAPTER THREE

Lessons

There were African Americans who called themselves Muslims in 1930s Detroit, but Betty Dean Sanders didn't know about them. My mother grew up sheltered in the perfectly conventional, solidly black, middle-class, firmly Christian household of her informally adoptive parents Lorenzo Don and Helen Malloy. There was no talk of black nationalism, no discussion of Islam as a viable religion for African Americans, no talk even of the pain and damage and anguish of racism. The Malloys, like many loving black parents of that time, thought the best way to arm their only child against racism was to teach her to ignore it.

Even after my mother graduated from high school and prepared to leave home to attend Tuskegee Institute in Alabama, a deeply southern and notoriously racist state, the Malloys could not bring themselves to speak the unspeakable. It wasn't until the day of my mother's departure that Grandmother Malloy finally tried to speak about racism. "My mother was at the train station . . . trying to mumble something," Betty said later. "Whatever she was trying to tell me, she was not very good at it and I laughed to myself. She was [usually] a bundle of confidence, and here she was just tripping over her words." Grandmother Malloy never managed to find the right words to prepare her daughter for what lay ahead.

"But the minute I got off that train, I knew what she was trying to say," my mother said. "She was trying to tell me in ten words or less about racism."

What exactly happened to my mother in Alabama, I do not know. Probably it was simply the everyday, routine degradation of finding oneself a second-class citizen in the greatest democracy on earth: "colored" water fountains and waiting rooms, divided towns and restaurants, lowered eyes and casual epithets, and beneath all interaction between whites and blacks a current of tension and hostility and fear. Whatever it was, the experience tilled the soil of my mother's imagination for the seeds my father would later sow in her mind.

After a year at Tuskegee my mother reconsidered her surroundings and plans to teach. She decided that nursing was her true calling and, with the blessings of her parents, transferred out of the south to the Brooklyn State Hospital School of Nursing, a Tuskegee-affiliated program in New York City. It was there, during her junior year, that a nurse's aide who worked at the hospital one day invited her to dinner at her apartment. The food was delicious, more complex and highly seasoned than anything my mother had tasted back in Detroit. After dinner, the friend invited my mother to attend a lecture at what was then called Temple No. 7 in Harlem. It would later be called Mosque No. 7.

"Now, how are you going to sit and eat all the food and say no?"

my mother wrote in *Essence* magazine years later. "So we went to the lecture, which I hoped would be over any minute. The woman wanted me to meet her minister, but he was not there that night."

My mother's friend wanted her to join the mosque, but my mother was not enthusiastic about the idea. "Number one, I was not familiar with the philosophy, and number two, my parents would kill me if they knew I joined another religion and gave up being a Methodist."

But she was enthusiastic about her friend's cooking, and because she wanted to sample it again, she felt she had to go hear her friend's minister. So she returned to Temple No. 7, and this time the dynamic young minister was present. His name was Malcolm X. Betty Dean Sanders was impressed. At another meeting some weeks later this man would be the first person to help my mother understand the discrimination she had experienced in Alabama. Less than two years later they were married. And along we came.

When my father left the Nation and converted to orthodox Islam, my mother converted, too. Together they deepened their study of the Qur'an and the teachings of the Prophet Mohammad. They realized that what they knew of as Islam from the teachings of Elijah Muhammad was really a stew of orthodox Islam, black nationalism, fanciful science, and fanciful history. They decided to pursue the Islam practiced by billions of people all over the world and become Sunni Muslims.

The basic creed of Islam is brief. There is no God but Allah, who is compassionate and just, and Muhammad is the prophet of Allah. Islam means surrender or submission. Muslims are those who have submitted themselves to the will of God in the name of peace and accept and proclaim the oneness of God.

When my father was assassinated, some people might have expected my mother to return to the Christian faith of her youth. Instead, she moved deeper into the faith of her choice. My mother was a devout Muslim; not many people realize that because she was extremely private about her faith. She did not proselytize. She did not wear the hijab—the traditional headcovering—in her everyday life, though she dressed modestly as the Qur'an instructs and was always appropriately covered in the mosque. My mother insisted on approaching Islam in a conservative manner. She did not believe Islam required women to be passive creatures locked away in a house somewhere. She believed she had the support of her religion in doing what she had to do—go out into the world and achieve for herself and for the sake of her family, just as millions of Muslims around the world do. And as she did so, she strove to fulfill the five pillars of Islam: she was conscious of Allah, she prayed, she fasted, she made hajj, and she gave generously, to individuals and to charity. I cannot count the number of stories I've heard about my mother leaving an envelope full of cash with someone in need, or a bag of clothes or goods with someone else. Mommy was also modest, she was a good person, and she stood up for her beliefs. She kept the Qur'an in a place of honor and reference in our home.

Islam was a shining, powerful force that sustained my mother through the darkest periods of her life, and she wanted her daughters to grow up with that same sustenance. So every Sunday, rain or shine, we went to the mosque.

It didn't matter what we'd done the night before—spent Saturday busy with lessons, gone to someone's party, or stayed up late watching movies on television. It didn't matter if we clung to our blankets and moaned and begged and whined to stay home, *Please, Mommy, please, just this once.* It didn't matter at all. My mother didn't even argue with us; that we were going to the mosque was just understood. She would rise and set about making oatmeal in the kitchen while the six of us dressed and combed our hair. As required, we dressed modestly and conservatively: ankle-length skirts, pants, or dresses, loose blouses, coverings for our heads.

When we were very young, we would be ferried into New York, often in a limousine. I'm sure some people at the mosque saw us piling out of that limo and thought we were rich, but during those first years after my father was assassinated, my mother was understandably cautious about driving herself and her six children into the city alone. Later, as years passed and fears eased, we would simply pile into my mother's car for the trip to the mosque. We all had our assigned seats: Malaak and I sat up front with my mother. Since I was older than Malaak, the window was mine. Qubilah had the driver's side window in the back and Attallah claimed the other window, with Gamilah and Malikah in between.

We attended the mosque at the Islamic Center, first on West 72nd Street and Riverside Drive and later, when the community moved, at East 97th Street and Third Avenue. The congregation was mostly foreign-born—people from the Sudan, Ethiopia, Somalia, Saudi Arabia, Pakistan, Egypt, the Philippines, or elsewhere in the world who had come to New York seeking a better life like so many immigrants before them. Our family was one of only a handful of African Americans who belonged to the mosque, but it was never an issue for us—or anyone else that we knew of. True Islam teaches the brotherhood of all people, and that's the way my mother genuinely raised us.

The first thing we did when we arrived at the mosque was to re-move our shoes and head upstairs to Qur'anic studies, a kind of Sunday school for Muslims. For the first hour of class, we studied the Qur'an; in the second hour, we learned how to read, write, and understand Arabic. At 12:30 P.M. we were allowed a break, espe-cially if we were going to be at the mosque the whole day. We'd burst forth from the doors like wild horses unleashed and race across the street to the park or up to the corner store for candy. My mother, as a rule, did not allow us to have much candy. Being a nurse and a Muslim, she was extremely health-conscious and care-fully monitored what we ate. But on Sundays we could sometimes sneak a few pieces of candy from the store.

After the break, the muezzin would sound the call and we would head back inside to perform our cleansing before beginning con-gregational prayer. Prayer began with the Imam, our prayer leader, standing at the front of the mosque facing toward Mecca, the holy city of Islam. We all lined up in rows behind him, men in front, women behind them, and children at the back. We tried as hard as we could to concentrate on the service, but as the prayers went on and on—standing, kneeling, lying prostrate—we sometimes let our attention wander. One thing I know: It's hard to be a child facing row upon row of bare adult feet with their accumulated bunions and corns and stubby toes and not giggle a little bit.

After mosque my mother would take us out to eat; this, for me, was the best part of the day. New York was and is a smorgasbord of possibilities, and my mother wanted us to sample as many as possible. We might have bagels and lox in a deli on the Upper West Side, dim sum in Chinatown, or dinner at an Indian or Ethiopian restaurant. After eating, if it was still early enough, she would take us to a concert or to Broadway to see a play.

Now, of course, I understand that she wanted us exposed to the world of fine arts, wanted us to learn to appreciate theater and performance and music of all kinds. And I enjoyed some of the cultural events. I loved seeing the beautiful dancers in the Alvin Ailey company fly their way across the stage. I liked the circus and I enjoyed magic shows. I liked musicals; I remember seeing *The Wiz* and feeling exhilarated by the soulful music and energetic dancing. And plays could also be interesting. Though once, when I was eight or nine, we went to see *The River Niger*. I remember having only a vague idea of what was going on—there was lots of cursing and sexual grunts—and after awhile my mother simply stood up and led us from the theater. We looked like ducklings, the six of us, dutifully following our mother duck all in a line. Poor Attallah must have been about thirteen and so tall and terribly embarrassed, but I was just as happy not to have to sit and listen anymore.

Classical music was the hardest of all; I just didn't have the musical sophistication to appreciate it. It was so much boring-if-pretty noise to me; I would have been happier just playing in our backyard. I would fidget in my seat, stare up at the glass chandeliers, shove my sister's elbow from the shared armrest, search the other faces in the audience, look pleadingly back up at whatever action was occurring onstage, all the while silently begging whoever controlled such things to let the torture end. *How much longer is this going to last?*

Going to the mosque every Sunday was such a routine part of our life that it never occurred to me that it was different, in some ways, from what most of my friends did on that day. When I was older, my friends asked why I prayed to Allah instead of God. I had to tell them that Allah was simply the Arabic word for God, that Allah *is* God, and then I realized we were something of a minority in this regard. But it was a good minority, an abundant one because we could attend and enjoy both mosque and church, whereas most of my friends only attended church.

My sisters and I all took our cue from Mommy, who, although a devout Muslim, never stressed the differences between Islam and Christianity, especially not among friends and family. As the Reverend Willie Barrow wrote, my mother used to say to her: "Girl, don't start talking to me about these sects and orders. Yeah, I'm a Muslim and you're a Church of God, but I'm going to the same place you're going."

Still, there are very real and significant differences between Islam and Christianity. As a child I was not aware of these deep, theological schisms, but I was aware of something else: Christians celebrated Christmas. We did not, but that didn't make us immune to the relentless marketing of that holiday. I'm sure we asked our mother more than once why we would not be receiving bunches of presents on Christmas Day like all our friends. And one year my three younger sisters and I decided to test the Santa Claus theory for ourselves.

My mother just happened to have in the house a three-foot-tall Christmas tree made out of porcelain. I think it was either a gift or a decoration for the day care center in which she was involved at the time. At any rate, on the night before Christmas, Gamilah, Malikah, Malaak, and I snuck out of bed after Mommy was asleep, found this tree, and pulled it from its box.

We set the tree up in the living room and surrounded it with the most Christmasy stuff we could find—decorations we'd made in school or cards people had sent us or anything. We found four sweatsocks and hung them on the fireplace. Then we went back to bed. Early the next morning we all jumped up and ran into the living room, expecting a Christmas wonderland. But there was no change. We were all so disappointed. I don't remember if we cried, but I know that was the last mention of Santa Claus in our house.

For us, December meant Qubilah's birthday. Birthdays were very special in our house. On our birthdays we always had cake and ice cream, balloons and presents, parties or a special dinner out. Even after we were grown and out of the house, Mommy continued to make our birthdays special. During my first year in college she drove up with the twins for my birthday party, bringing with her flowers wrapped with a beautiful ribbon on which was inscribed, *Ilyasah's Birthday, July 22, 1979.*

But for a Muslim child the most notable observance of the year is Ramadan.

Ramadan is the holiest month of the Islamic year, a period of introspection and prayer that recalls the receiving of the Qur'an. During Ramadan, able-bodied adults and older children fast during daylight hours, from dawn to dusk. It is a time of communal prayer in the mosque and the reading of the Qur'an. It is a time for conscientiously refraining not only from food and drink during the day, but also from all kinds of immoral behavior—lying, cheating, hurting other human beings. Still, Ramadan is less a period of atonement than an obedient response to God's holy commandment. It is a time for forgiveness of sins.

During Ramadan we rose each morning before the sun to have breakfast. The Qur'an says eating and drinking are permissible only until the "white thread of light becomes distinguishable from the dark thread of night at dawn." And so after sunrise we fasted for the remainder of the day. Because we were children we were allowed to drink water when necessary.

After sunset every evening we would say special prayers before breaking our fasts with dates and water. Then we would have dinner, plates and plates of healthy, delicious food like lean meats, sweet potatoes and other vegetables, salads, fresh fruits, and plenty of fresh-baked breads.

At the end of the thirty-day period we would celebrate with the festival of Eid Mubarak, the Feast of Fast-Breaking. One of my favorite Eid celebrations took place when I was ten or eleven. All the African American families from our mosque gathered at the home of a family named Kareem. We arrived before sunset to prepare for our evening prayers and then the feast began. There was so much food my stomach roared just looking at it.

By the time I was old enough to realize that many of my neighborhood and school friends did not observe Ramadan, it was so much a part of our life, so firmly established a routine, that it didn't seem like any big deal. Fasting did not make me feel different from other children and I neither dreaded it nor fought it. On the other hand, not being able to eat our housekeeper's delicious cupcakes sure wasn't anything I looked forward to.

My mother raised us as Muslims, but she also wanted us to have respect for the Christian beliefs held by members of both her adoptive and real families. The Malloys, her adoptive parents who lived in Detroit, were strong, solid Christians. Mommy's biological father, Shelman Sanders, with whom she remained close, and his family were likewise devoted Christians and churchgoers in their Philadelphia community. One of my mother's half brothers, Uncle Stanley, eventually had his own church.

Whenever we visited my grandparents in Philadelphia during the summer, we would get up every Sunday and go with them to Friendship Baptist Church. My sisters tolerated these Sundays, but I reveled in them. I loved church, loved everything about it. I loved sitting in the pews, watching the women stream down the aisle in their Sunday finery. I loved the praying and the testifying and the joyfulness. Most of all I loved the gospel music and the spirited singing and clapping that went on in church. It seemed to me a living, breathing manifestation of all the African American history my mother made certain we learned. I would sit in the pews, swaying to the music, lost in a reverie about my ancestors, all those strong people of African descent who survived the terrors of slavery through the sheer strength of their own will and created the gospel hymns. I loved it so much I'd sometimes close my eyes and try to get the spirit myself. I wanted to feel whatever powerful force was causing all of these people to sing and clap so heartily. I never did catch the spirit, but I always kept the hope.

After services, we would all return to my grandparents' house for Sunday dinner and rest. Later on that evening, when my grandmother asked if any of us children wanted to accompany Uncle

John or Uncle Stanley back to church for evening service, I always volunteered. My sisters thought I was crazy. Going back to church? Voluntarily? They shook their heads and rolled their eyes and giggled and called me Christian girl. But I didn't care. I got to dress up and be with my southern kin. I got to hear the power of my people transformed into song.

Among the other African American families at our mosque were the Yobas, whose son Malik is now an actor, best known for his starring role on the television series "New York Undercover." There was also a family named Kareem; their son, Gamal, was my first boyfriend. We met when I was six years old. He was about the same age as I and looked like Michael Jackson, who, at the time, was my idea of a dream date. All the girls liked Gamal, but for some reason he chose me to be his girlfriend. Not that being his girlfriend entailed very much—the occasional shared piece of chocolate or affectionate pop in the arm.

Then one day, when I was eleven years old, Gamal apparently decided it was time to take our relationship up a notch. During a break at the mosque, he began chasing me and, not knowing what else to do, I ran. I headed for the ramp linking the top of the mosque to the bottom. It was a long, curving ramp, something like the one at the Guggenheim Museum in New York. By the time we ran all the way down I was exhausted, and not even sure what I was running from. But then Gamal caught up to me and kissed me on the cheek. It was my first kiss of any kind from a boy, and I wasn't ready. I told Gamal we were finished. He took it with aplomb, and a few weeks later he had a new girlfriend, a friend of mine named Suhailah.

One day we heard the Kareems were going to Africa. Now, despite my mother's educational efforts, we were still average American children. Meaning we watched Saturday afternoon television like everyone else, we saw those movies of Tarzan swinging through the jungle like some loin-clothed superhero while the Africans ran around with bones in their noses, scared of their own shadows, trying to catch some poor defenseless white woman and boil her for lunch. Africa did not seem like the safest place to be. So when I heard the Kareems were going there, I ran to my mother, alarmed.

"Mommy! The Kareems are going to Africa!"

"I know. Isn't it exciting?"

No, it wasn't exciting. It was scary. Africa was full of vicious lions and bug-eyed folks with spears. And worse, there were no grocery stores. "Will the Kareems be able to eat chocolate?" I asked my mother. This was a big concern of mine. Chocolate was very important to me.

"They'll be able to eat chocolate if they want."

"Where will they live? In huts?"

"No, they will not live in huts. They will live in a house."

"Is there water? Will they have clothes?"

It wasn't as though I was completely ignorant about the motherland. My father, of course, had traveled the continent extensively before his death, and even said that were it not for his commitment to the struggle at home he would have stayed in Africa. My mother had filled our home with books about Africa, with paintings and fine wood carvings from that continent. We had, probably more than most black children of my generation, a sense of Africa as a noble, enlightened place of great history, not as the third world but the first world, the place where civilization began.

Still, there were those Tarzan movies. There were those skillfully created images of Africans running through the forest like bug-eyed madmen that had been indelibly etched into my mind. And once those images are present inside your head, they are hard to erase. Especially if you're eight years old.

"Yes, sweetheart," my mother said gently. "The Kareems will have plenty of clothes in Africa, beautiful clothes made of elegant fabric like you've never seen."

This is about the time we began having tutors.

I don't mean to make it sound as though my mother suddenly woke up one day and realized she needed to steer our educational course very closely. That's not true at all. Education was always an important part of Betty Dean Sanders Shabazz's life. Her adoptive mother was a schoolteacher, her adoptive father a college graduate and owner of a shoe-repair business, who often said that it was education that enabled him to carve out a comfortable middle-class existence despite the Great Depression. Like so many African Americans of their generation and before, the Malloys—both graduates of Tuskegee—viewed education as vitally important for black people. It was the key to financial security and independence, the cornerstone of self-respect and dignity, the means of lifting a people from oppression and poverty. And unlike fame or favor or even wealth, education was immutable. Once acquired, it could not be taken away.

Likewise, my father believed strongly in the importance of education. One of my greatest concerns about the way my family's history is told is the distorted picture that is given of my father's

early years and his family, especially his mother. Many people believe she broke down under the weight of family responsibility
because she was a fair-skinned, fragile West Indian woman. They
think that before Malcolm Little went to prison and discovered Elijah Muhammad he was an illiterate thug who could barely sign his
name. Even I had this impression as an adolescent.

To some degree, the *Autobiography* itself is responsible for this
myth. My father, remorseful about his criminal behavior and grateful and utterly devoted to Mr. Muhammad, downplayed his own
intelligence and his family's educational and moral influence.

But the truth is, the Littles were dignified, professional, and up-
standing citizens, and it was they who instilled their values in young
Malcolm. The Reverend Earl Little was a Baptist minister who
helped organize Marcus Garvey's United Negro Improvement Association. His mother, Louise Norton Little, was an educated woman
from Grenada who spoke five languages and served as recording secretary for the United Negro Improvement Association. As a young
mother, she filled the house with language and culture and the love
of education, teaching her children to sing the alphabet in French
and having them read to her from newspapers produced by Garvey
and a fellow Grenadian, Theophilus Albert Marryshow. She kept a
dictionary on the table where her children did their homework, and
if they mispronounced a word, she made them look it up. It was
Grandmother Louise and Reverend Little who sowed the seeds of
insight, discipline, educational values, and organizational skills in my
father, not Elijah Muhammad. Mr. Muhammad cleared away the
weeds and allowed those seeds to flourish and grow.

My father himself was president of his all-white seventh-grade class. His teenage letters to his sister Ella in Boston show an articulate, charming, and intelligent young man with excellent writing skills. As a youth, Malcolm Little aspired to a career in the law—until a white teacher discouraged him, saying black people were more suited to menial jobs.

That discouragement led him to drop out of school, which in turn led to a life of petty crime. Society taught Detroit Red how to debase himself. When he ended up in prison at the age of twenty-one, and had time to reflect, he returned to the moral principles of his youth because his favorite brother, Reginald, told him of a "Black Messiah," reminding him of the seeds his parents had planted. He resumed a lifelong program of self-education. He fed his hungry intellect with newspapers, magazines, biographies, histories, the dictionary, the encyclopedia—anything on which he could get his hands. After he joined the Nation of Islam, his reading became more directed but no less voracious. He had a wide range of interests: the classics, anthropology, African history, the origins of religion, anything by or about people of color. He could polish off weighty tomes in three hours, and easier ones in one or two. He was so widely read and so brilliant that people, later, would not believe he had never graduated high school. "Education is an important element in the struggle for human rights," he said. "It is the means to help our children and our people rediscover their identity and thereby increase self-respect." He also said, "Education is our passport to the future," and that "tomorrow belongs to those who truly prepare for it today."

So there was never any question in our house but that we girls would receive the broadest and best education possible. As it turned out, that education took place in schools that were predominantly white. Not so long ago I was talking to a friend who, reflecting upon this aspect of my childhood, shook his head in surprise. "You know, Ilyasah," he said, "it's almost a contradiction for you and your sisters to have gone to predominantly white schools."

It wasn't the first time I've heard such a sentiment, and it probably won't be the last. But it just goes to show how some people don't understand what Betty Shabazz stood for. And it just goes to show how some people do not understand Malcolm X and his message. I wonder what these people who were surprised by my having attended private schools think Mommy should have done. Should she have enrolled us in some underfunded public school where too many of our children are having their bright minds dulled by watered-down academics and low expectations? To do so would have been contrary to my father's legacy.

My mother worked hard to send her daughters to the best schools she could find: We attended Montessori schools in the elementary grades; Attallah, Gamilah, and Qubilah attended the United Nations International School in Manhattan; and Malikah and Malaak were sent to the Thornton-Donovan School in New Rochelle. After primary school, I went on to the Masters School in Dobbs Ferry and Hackley Preparatory School in Tarrytown. All this effort on Mommy's part had nothing to do with social status. It had nothing to do with wanting to be around white people. Mommy did what she did because she knew we had to be one step ahead both educationally and culturally in a society that had been historically unjust. She believed arming us with education and self-knowledge was a necessity if we were to have sound and fulfilling futures in America.

———

But Mommy knew, too, that just sending us to good private schools was not enough. She knew she would have to supplement our education in the areas where these schools were sadly deficient: the history and importance of Africans and African Americans. My mother wanted us to grow up with a love of the motherland, with the knowledge of how Africa gave birth to thriving civilizations, with a deep sense of pride in our family, our culture, and our people of the African diaspora.

This, after all, was the effort to which my father had dedicated his life: self-empowerment; opening the eyes of black Americans to their own true greatness. This was my father's greatest gift to people of African descent in America, this liberation from the self-loathing branded into our souls by four hundred years of racism and oppression. It's easy to forget now, but in 1952, when my father left prison and joined the Nation's Temple No. 1 in Detroit, black was not considered beautiful. It was, "If you're light, you're all right. If you're brown, stick around. If you're black, get back." That was the way far too many of us viewed ourselves.

My father used to say the biggest difference between the parallel oppression of the modern Jews and of blacks was that "Jews never lost pride in being Jewish." They knew they made a significant contribution to the world, and they vowed never to forget. They teach their children history and culture at a very young age, because they know the knowledge of one's history is absolutely critical.

Don't believe it? Why then do goverments spend millions upon millions of dollars building monuments? Why did the apartheid government of South Africa lie to generations of indigenous South Africans, teaching them they came from the Netherlands as slaves to the Dutch? My father said, "It is the process of mis-education that inhibits the full potential of a nation." History grounds a people. It reminds them of their past and encourages belief in their future. History is empowermen, and we as a people should want to empower ourselves.

We should teach our children their history and not rely on anyone else. But to do that, we have to first know who we are. At a time when African Americans were full of confusion and self-loathing about the color of their skin and the curl of their hair, Malcolm X stood up and declared that we were not Negroes but that we were first and foremost Africans, people of African descent. And we should be proud of that fact. Our heritage was stripped from us—if Italian Americans go to Italy and German Americans go to Germany, where do Negroes go? Negroland? Blackland?—but we could reclaim it. We must reclaim it.

"Just because you take a zebra and put it in France, that doesn't make it French," Daddy used to say. "It's still a zebra."

So, on Wednesday afternoons, Brother K. Ahamad Tawfiq came to our house to teach us Arabic and to lecture us about the Qur'an and Africa. He was a sheik, the Imam of the Mosque of Islamic Brotherhood in New York, and a wonderful storyteller. We would sit on the floor in the dining room, after carefully writing out our Arabic lessons for the day, and listen as Brother Tawfiq wove stories of ancient kings and queens and great kingdoms. Before I learned about Dick, Jane, and Spot, I learned about Marcus Garvey, Nat Turner, and Frederick Douglass. Before I learned about the American Revolution, I learned about how Toussaint L'Ouverture and the slaves of Haiti overthrew their oppressors and claimed their freedom and their land. I learned about King Tut. I learned about the true ethnicity of the great Egyptian pharaoh Djoser and the brilliant architect, astronomer, and physician Imhotep who built his tomb.

I learned that four thousand years before the birth of Christ, the civilization of Nubia, Sudan of Ethiopia, gave rise to the nation of Egypt, which in turn gave rise to the great civilization of Greece. We learn all about Greece in our history lessons at school, but little about Egypt and nothing about Nubia.

Through Brother Tawfiq, Mommy addressed the institutional notion that one ethnic group was superior to another. Because any time we are taught that Cleopatra resembles Elizabeth Taylor as opposed to Lauryn Hill, or that Moses resembles Charlton Heston as opposed to Frederick Douglass, Benjamin Banneker, Tupac, or any young African American man walking proudly down the street, then we know our education is denying us opportunity for growth. Such teaching denies America's children self-love and prevents collective respect for human life and achievement. It is a disservice to humanity.

Listening to Brother Tawfiq, I learned my true heritage. And so I was armed when presented with a white-washed view of history.

Once, when I was about nine years old, one of my teachers at the St. Joseph Montessori School began a history lesson about Christopher Columbus. With a warm smile on her face she told us how, in 1492, Columbus sailed the ocean blue and discovered this great land of America. All the other children nodded but I raised my hand. I was confused, and my mother had taught me to ask questions when I felt that way.

"Miss Hawthorne? How could Columbus discover a place where

people were already living?" Miss Hawthorne smiled but did not address my question. She said we were following the text.

History lessons at school often left me befuddled. At home I was learning about a place called Africa, a land that was beautiful and colorful and grand in the full sense of the word, a proud and ancient continent of thriving societies and happy people. In school, the only thing I learned about Africans or African Americans was that George Washington Carver invented the peanut and Martin Luther King had a dream and wanted black kids and white kids to hold hands. There was no grandeur, no sense of achievement or accomplishment at all. The version of history I learned made my people seem very, very small.

When my teacher began talking about the first columns and the first arches and how architecture began in Greece, I just stared at her. How could those Greek buildings, as pretty as they were, be the first great architecture when there were these other magnificent structures, these great stone pyramids rising up along the Nile thousands of years before? When I asked these questions of Miss Hawthorne she ignored them.

"We're going by the text," she said.

But Brother Tawfiq did not ignore my questions. He told me the truth of my heritage. Sitting on that dining room floor I envisioned this beautiful place called Africa, a land of peace and culture and dignity and great happiness. Brother Tawfiq and his stories left me with a great sense of imagination and pride. And I can still read and write Arabic.

But our after-school activities didn't stop with black history. We studied French, with Attallah and Qubilah quickly becoming fluent. We took lessons in yoga, ballet, and African dance. We studied music, as my father would have wanted. He loved all kinds of music, from classical to soul, and he believed the study of jazz, especially, taught precision, poise, timing, and coordination. Not to mention pride.

My mother also got us involved with the local chapter of Jack and Jill. Jack and Jill of America is an organization founded by Marion Stubbs Thomas, a music teacher, and a group of other African American mothers in Philadelphia in 1938. The mothers were seeking to provide a wealth of cultural, social, and recreational experiences for their children in a segregated and often hostile world. News of this new organization spread fast and chapters developed in nearby cities. Jack and Jill of America was incorporated under the laws of the state of Delaware in 1946.

The organization soon came to mean not only cultural and social opportunities, but community service. With the goal "to seek for all children the same advantages we desire for our own," chapters to this day adopt projects, conduct fund-raisers, and contribute to organizations such as the Children's Defense Fund and the NAACP.

What all this meant for us was bake sales, ski getaways, raffles, and parties with other middle-class African American children. I remember one of the first events I attended was a party at someone's house in Bronxville. The family was very wealthy and the house was beautiful. When we arrived the parents were all milling about upstairs. We children were ushered downstairs into the basement, a beautiful recreation room decorated in black and white. Music was playing on the stereo and the children, teenagers older than myself, were dancing closely on the dance floor. I stared at them in awe.

Some people consider organizations such as Jack and Jill elitist. Attallah, for one, wasn't interested in the group; she didn't care for the emphasis on social standing and the way some members displayed a kind of colorism snobbery.

But Mommy, who was mahogany brown and proud of it and far from a snob, wasn't in it for that. The truth is she was very active in social causes. The people who join Jack and Jill want their children to play with other children for whom education and ambition haven't been made "uncool." Also, I believe Jack and Jill is important because when you are a person of color growing up in an affluent community, nine times out of ten you don't come into contact with other African Americans. You either start thinking you're better than less affluent African Americans or you simply don't think of yourself as black at all. You start recalling the fifth-generation Irish and Native American bloodline—anything except the obvious African. Jack and Jill helps counteract those beliefs.

At the same time, Mommy believed in the ability of organizations such as Jack and Jill to channel the talents and resources of middle-class African Americans toward uplifting the race. You didn't just join the Links, an organization of African American women, to party, you funded scholarships and mentored children and affected policy. Together you reached back and pulled up, locally, nationally, and abroad. And in doing so you not only made a solid contribution to society, but you served as an inspiration and role model. It's good for African American children to see people who look like them helping them.

That was why my mother brought me into the Links in 1992. I'll admit that at first, seeing all these society women in their big hats and bigger cocktail rings, I was unsure about becoming a member of such a group. But when I heard them really talking about issues and offering possible solutions, I realized that these were people who were clearly capable of helping others, and that's when I said I wanted to join.

In many ways my sisters and I lived a life of privilege, and I suppose we took it for granted, as children will. I grew up largely unaware of that other world of black America in which children study no music and attend deteriorating public schools and live in cramped apartments in violent neighborhoods. My mother neither went out of her way to show us this world nor tried to keep us from seeing it. She knew we would learn of our people's condition soon enough. Our job was to prepare ourselves.

People often ask me what it was like to grow up in a house full of girls. It's hard for me to answer that question, since I, of course, don't have any other upbringing with which to compare it. The best I can say is that it was the absolute greatest. We had lots of fun, my sisters and I. We had it all, at home—all the friends anyone would wish for, plus more friends in our neighborhood, at our mosque, at the homes of our relatives. There was never a lonely moment in our house. Attallah and Qubilah hung out together and the four youngest girls did everything together. Growing up in a house full of women prepares you to get along with other women, and teaches you how to be a good friend. That's something all women need.

Attallah, whose name means "Gift of God," is the firstborn. Being the oldest child gave her a certain weight and responsibility. She was bright, assured, observant. At five she taught our twelve-year-old baby-sitter, Gail, a prayer in Arabic, drilling Gail until she got it right.

Attallah was also the comedian in the family, the entertainer, the dramatic one. (She was also the one who people thought looked most like my father, because her sandy hair and cafe-au-lait coloring is the same as his. But Mommy would say Attallah really looks more like her, while Malikah and I look most like our dad.)

Attallah would come into our room in the mornings, after our housekeeper had tried and failed to wake us, and perform her own one-woman show. She'd come to the door of the bedroom I shared with Gamilah and knock.

"Who is it?" Knock, knock.

"Who is it?" Knock, knock.

Feigning exasperation, "Who is it, I say?!"

Then she'd swagger into the room, hitching up her pants like John Wayne. "It's me, pilgrim. I come to fix the sink."

"What sink?"

"The sink you said was clogged, pilgrim!"

"I never called about a sink! I don't know what you mean."

"Oh Duke! I'm the one who called!"

And on and on, switching voices, gesturing wildly until Gamilah and I were rolling on our beds, convulsed in laughter, fully awake. Sometimes Attallah would include, in the middle of her show, a breakdancing routine. She knew all the latest dances—the funky chicken, the bump. She could get down with the best of them, dancing there before us, her big, sandy-colored Afro waving in the breeze. Rerun had nothing on her. It was Attallah who got us into the ritual of watching "Soul Train" every Saturday morning. Afterward my sisters and I would gather in the kitchen and perform an enthusiastic dance routine while singing the Sister Sledge song "We Are Family." I was always Kathie Sledge.

Qubilah is the second oldest; her name means "Mother Nature." Qubilah is the brain of the family. As a child she loved science and nature and finding out why things worked the way they did. She was the one who thought making a volcano from baking soda and vinegar was cool. She liked to gather my younger sisters and me into the hallway, close all the doors so that it was very dark, then chomp on wintergreen Lifesavers and make sparks fly out of her mouth while we looked on in awe. She seemed to me a stone-cold genius; everything she did was so smart. She often tried to help me with my homework, explaining why it was that x equaled y plus 2, but I'd just look at her in amazement. Half the time I had no idea what she was talking about.

One time she brought home a shoe box full of strange items that looked like dried weeds or large, hairy mothballs. She put them in her nightstand, near her pet turtle, and went on about her way. It turned out the "weeds" were really cocoons and a few weeks later we had all manner of insect life hatching in our house. Our mother was not amused.

Gamilah ("Beautiful") Lamumba was probably the most popular among us. She was the one all the kids in the neighborhood liked, the one everybody wanted to be friends with. Gamilah was always down.

Gamilah was also our living *TV Guide*. She liked reading and read every book in our study, but she *loved* television, especially Saturday morning shows like "Abbott and Costello," "Little Rascals," and those old spaghetti westerns. If you wanted to know what was on television at any given moment, all you had to do was ask Gamilah. Even if she wasn't allowed to watch a program, she somehow knew about it.

Gamilah and I shared a room in which everything was identical. We had the same beds, the same dressers, the same teal-and-blue comforters. The only difference was Gamilah did not often keep her side of the room up to my standards of orderliness. She wasn't sloppy, just more casual than I about hanging up her clothes and picking up her things. I was a fanatic about orderliness.

One day I just got fed up. My mother and older sisters were out of the house somewhere, and although my mother had not actually put me in charge, I assumed the position anyway. When Gamilah announced that she was going outside to play with her friends, I shook my head.

"Not until you clean up your side of the room," I said.

"Says who?"

"Says me."

My sister crossed her arms and tossed her head. "Who died and made you king?"

I ignored her and gestured at the rumpled bed. "You need to pick up your clothes and make your bed and straighten up the place. Then, maybe, I'll let you go."

Gamilah laughed. "Are you kidding? I'm going out."

She began walking toward the door but stopped when I blocked her path. I was always big for my age, and Gamillah was almost two years younger than I. She was not going to challenge me directly and we both knew it. All I had to do was approach her and she would back down onto the bed and kick her feet in the air with a girly grin.

"Clean the room," I said, using my most authoritative voice. "Then you can go out."

She fussed and fumed for a while but I just turned and left the room. And to make sure she stayed inside and did as told, I locked the door. "I'll let you out when that room is clean," I called to her. Feeling pretty proud of myself, I went downstairs and busied myself in the kitchen or the living room or something. Maybe fifteen minutes later I decided she'd had enough time and went back up to our room.

"Are you finished?" I called through the closed door. No answer. Gamilah was still sulking like a child. I opened the door. Gamilah was gone.

For a moment I just stood in the doorway, too stunned to think straight. How could she have gotten past a locked door? Did she have a key I didn't know about? Then I noticed one of the windows was open. I broke all speed records running across that room, already envisioning my sister's crumpled body thirty feet below in the backyard. But Gamilah had tied several sheets together, tied the end to the cast-iron window frames, and climbed down the improvised rope. I was both furious and relieved to look out that window and see no sign of her down below. I don't remember what happened when she finally came back from playing with her friends. Probably our mother was home by then and so I let it go.

Then there were the twins, Malikah ("Queen") Saban and Malaak ("Angel") Saban, born six minutes apart, seven months after my father died. I adored the twins as babies. They were like little dolls to me, dolls that could open their eyes and shove their fat little fingers into their mouths and stick their butts in the air when they slept. I thought they were so cute. They were always "the twins," always together and always dressed alike.

My mother, in her wisdom, paired us off, informally assigning each younger girl to an older girl for all-around watching, nurturing, and bonding. Malaak was Attallah's baby. Malikah was Qubilah's. They got to hold them, comfort them, give them their bottles, change their clothes. Gamilah was supposed to be "my baby," but she was only two years younger than I and seemed decidedly un-doll-like to me.

As they grew older, Malikah was very sweet and smart, a real whiz. She was also a bit of a tattletale until we taught her not to be that way. We never told on one another. Malaak was the younger of the two and those minutes made her the baby of the family. She was a demure, angelic, timid little girl, the one we sang songs to and looked after more than anyone else. Even though the twins each had their "assigned" big sister, it was really the four of us youngest who hung out together while Attallah and Qubilah were off doing their big-girl things. And that made me the oldest, the one in charge. I always thought I was in charge. I was the self-appointed mother of the younger three.

Attallah and Malaak shared a room, Qubilah and Malikah shared a room, and I shared a room with Gamilah. Our room was upstairs and had probably served as the maid's quarters when Congresswoman Bella Abzug lived in the house. It had its own bathroom and an enormous closet where Gamilah and I hung the posters of whoever we were in love with that month—the Silvers, James Brown, Chaka Kahn, the Jackson Five.

The others were passing fancies, but Michael Jackson held my heart all through childhood. I was a Michael Jackson fanatic. I remember sitting on the couch with my mother as she knitted a hat for me. We were watching the Ed Sullivan show when suddenly Michael Jackson and his brothers came on. I jumped up and squealed so loudly my mother almost had a heart attack. When I was eight or nine years old it occurred to me that Michael would probably love me back if he just knew I was alive. I decided to write him a letter. I told him my name and where I lived and how old I was. I told him my father was Malcolm X and my mother was Betty Shabazz; I figured that would at least get his attention. I wanted to know if I could come see him and become his friend. I mailed the letter with high hopes, but I never got a reply.

Being the third of six girls, I suppose I could be considered the middle child of the family. But middle children are supposed to be the lost ones, the daughters overlooked between the excited anticipation of the first child and the relaxed and joyful gushing over the baby. Middle children are supposed to wonder about their identity, their role in life. They're also supposed to be the peacemakers of the family. I'm not sure how much of that applies to me.

What I can say is that I was a rambunctious child, the kind who needed constant distraction in a restaurant to keep her from running into the kitchen and getting underfoot. I was feisty and tough, big for my age, with a deep voice to match. "You didn't let anybody push you around," our baby-sitter Gail said. "If I heard Gamilah crying, I knew it was you."

If I needed a hug or a kiss from Mommy, I went right up and took it. I had no qualms about making demands and asking questions and sharing my innermost desires and dreams with my mother.

There is a well-known photograph of my family with Muhammad Ali; they had to bribe me with candy for that picture, because I was not at all interested in sitting still. I exasperated my preschool teachers at the Headstart program by running around and generally ignoring whatever instructions they tried to give. If it was circle time, I wanted to go outside. If it was recess time, I wanted to sit in the doorway and play with my coat. If it was story time, I wanted to run laps around the room. I was so defiant I would get a spanking nearly every day when I came home.

My mother said the only person I ever listened to was my father; anyone else was just making noise in my ear. Even my mother had a hard time getting through. For example, I sucked my thumb until I was three years old. My mother tried everything she could think of to get me to stop. She tried demanding, she tried cajoling, she even tried hot sauce. But I just plopped my thumb into my mouth and sucked away, hot sauce or no. Everyone was amazed. They said I had no fear.

Looking back, I think I wasn't so much fearless or even defiant as grasping, trying to find my way. My mother did a superhuman job of cushioning us from the stinging pain of my father's absence. Daddy's death was never discussed. There was no therapy, no support group or books on death; we all had to find our own ways of dealing, even if subconsciously. Especially the three oldest of us.

Attallah, I think, dealt with it by being so much like my father: resilient, protective of loved ones, a natural and gifted leader. Qubilah coped by quietly retreating. Besides being so smart, she was, probably, the most sensitive of us. "If anyone was likely to get her feelings hurt, it was her," said our baby-sitter Gail. Qubilah went inside herself, just lowered the blinds, and kept her feelings to herself.

But me, I was very bold about getting my needs met. If I needed a hug, somebody was going to give me a hug or hear about it. If I felt lonely, if I wanted affection, I found a way to let people know. Sometimes a child can vocalize her emotions, put words to her needs; sometimes she can't. So she knocks over a lamp or makes a loud noise or drives the teacher to distraction. Either way, the cry is the same: Please pay attention to me. Every child needs and deserves as much love and presence as the adults in her life can muster up.

Camp Betsey Cox

Betsey Cox was a settler in pre-Revolutionary Vermont who had the misfortune of one day being kidnapped by a raiding party of local Indians. The kidnappers were reportedly accompanied by a disaffected white colonist, an American whose sympathies lay with the French. Their plan was to grab Betsey and her sister, Sarah June, take them over the border to Montreal, and ransom them off.

But things soon went awry. Sarah June escaped her captors and made her way into town to sound the alarm. The villagers responded with guns. The kidnappers found themselves with the entire village on their trail—and a large and possibly pregnant Betsey on their hands—and decided the better part of common sense was to abandon ship and Betsey, too.

For some reason, it was Betsey, and not the feisty Sarah June, who became famous afterward for surviving the raid. It was Betsey who was remembered, Betsey who had a mountain and a street named in her honor. And when my mother announced that Gamilah and I would be attending a summer camp in Vermont, it was Betsey Cox, and not the feisty Sarah June, whose name fell from her lips.

There's something to be said, I guess, for just living to tell the tale.

Of course, I had never heard of Camp Betsey Cox; I was seven years old and had scarcely heard of the state of Vermont. Certainly I had no real understanding of what a summer camp meant, namely that I would be spending weeks away from Mommy and sleeping with strangers for the first time in my life. I certainly didn't realize Gamilah and I would be the only black people in sight.

But who cared? It sounded exciting—marshmallows around the campfire, all the swimming and boating and arts and crafts you could stand. My mother had enrolled Attallah and Qubilah at the Farm and Wilderness Camp in another part of Vermont, so we were all caught up in the coming adventure.

On the appointed day my mother drove the four of us up to Vermont. She must have dropped Attallah and Qubilah off first, but I don't remember much about their new summer home. I was far too nervous. By now the reality of being separated from my mother for weeks had set in and I wasn't pleased with the notion. More than any of my sisters, I was a Mommy's girl. My mother was always the most important person in the world to me; I told her so from the time I could talk. *Mommy, I love you. Mommy, you're the most important person in the world to me. Mommy, if anything ever happens to you, I'll just crumble.* As I got older, my mother tried to gently redirect some of my intensity. "Yasah, you need to focus on yourself," she would tell me.

———

Camp Betsey Cox is built on the site of an old hill farm near Pitts-ford, Vermont. Surrounded by the Green Mountains, the property spans acres and acres of lush green meadowland and cool, dark, pine-needled woods. There are tennis courts; grooming stables and horseback riding paths; a huge vegetable patch; and a spring-fed lake. That first day, as we pulled off the main street and began trav-eling down the long, white gravel road, I could not believe my eyes. Gamilah and I were not in Mount Vernon anymore.

The cabins were named after Vermont mountains: Lincoln, Pico, Killington, Mansfield, Camels Hump. We were assigned to Sugar-bush. It was pretty rustic, with rough, pine-board walls, canvas bunks, and a huge stone fireplace. The showers and toilets were outside, a few yards away, in a wash house. We shared the cabin with six other girls and two counselors.

The counselors had names like Marci and Laurie and Chicky and Bess. They were all pretty white college girls with bare feet, long hair, and earnest smiles, and almost immediately I felt com-fortable among them. They approached Gamilah and me with warmth and openness. There was one in particular whom Gamilah and I came to love. Her name was Jenny, and she paid a lot of at-tention to us, seeking us out during the day or sitting with us at vespers after dark. Jenny had long, curly black hair and beautiful copper skin that darkened easily beneath the Vermont sun. I as-sumed, without ever really thinking about it, that Jenny was black. Later on we found out she was Jewish and lived in New York, not far from our mosque.

It wasn't until I became an adult that I learned some of the counselors were, in fact, quite nervous about our arrival that first year. They heard that the daughters of Malcolm X were coming to camp and some of them panicked. But Mike, the camp director and an admirer of my father's, reassured them that we were just kids, that there would be no fiery stares across the breakfast table, no name-calling in archery class, or fingers pointed accusingly across the campfire at night.

Part of their apprehension was just a sign of the times. It was the early seventies, and the country was still reeling from the sixties, with its wars and protests and political assassinations. Martin Luther King Jr. had been assassinated, and young African American activists, angered and frustrated with the slow pace of change, were growing more militant. Stokely Carmichael was preaching "black power." Out in Oakland, California, Bobby Seale and Huey Newton had formed the Black Panther Party for Self-Defense, taking my father's teachings as the basis of their philosophy. Eldridge Cleaver, who said he had "washed his hands in the blood of the martyr Malcolm X," had rocked mainstream white America with his groundbreaking prison memoir *Soul on Ice*. And America and the world had watched in shock as sprinters Tommie Smith and John Carlos stood on an Olympic medal stand in Mexico City and raised their black, gloved fists defiantly in the air.

These were tense, suspicious times between black people and white, and the counselors of Camp Betsey Cox could not possibly have been immune. It wasn't as though they had a lot of practice integrating black children into the camp, even black children who were not the daughters of outspoken and slain black heroes. Gamilah and I were among the first African American children to attend Betsey Cox, despite its long history. Whether this was due to the camp's failure to make itself known to black families, or the natural suspicions of black folks—*You want me to send my child where? To be watched by who?*—I don't know. Probably some of both.

But my mother was an educated and deeply spiritual woman who had faith in human kindness despite all that had happened to her. Plus she was a martyr's widow raising six girls on her own; the truth is, she needed a break and wanted to keep us busy. So she found the two best camps she could, negotiated a payment plan, trusted in Allah, and sent us off. I believe she chose well. In all my years at Camp Betsey Cox, I felt nothing but warmth and respect from the counselors and staff. So welcoming were they, and so sheltered was I from the racial turmoil of the times, that I did not even fully absorb until I was older, probably fourteen, the fact that Gamilah and I and a few other girls were the only black children at Camp Betsey Cox. In fact, the only racial incident I recall happened not at the camp itself, but in town.

It was the Fourth of July and all the girls at camp got dressed and went with their counselors into Pittsford to participate in the local parade. It was a big event, as parades in small towns often are. There were balloons and streamers and crowds. People lined up on either side of the main street, flags in hand, to watch the bands and high school floats and aging veterans march proudly past. We were all cheering with everyone else, when I noticed that some of the townspeople seemed to be staring at Gamilah and me and our friend Lisa Stroud, who is the daughter of the brilliant singer and performer Nina Simone. Now, of course, I realize that we were not just the only black faces in sight, we were probably the only black faces some of the townspeople had ever seen. But at the time, I had no idea what was going on. All I knew was that people were staring, grown-ups were staring, and they weren't supposed to stare. I squirmed a little, trying to inconspicuously check my clothes to make sure my underwear wasn't showing or my hair wasn't sticking up. Then the counselors seemed to notice. They moved closer to Gamilah and Lisa and me and put their arms around our shoulders. One of them muttered something under her breath. Then, out of nowhere, I felt a hand on my head. Someone from the crowd behind us had reached out to stroke my hair. By the time I turned around the hand was gone and I couldn't tell to which of the white faces behind me it had belonged. They were all staring; not wanting to stare back, I probably smiled. But over the fading music of the marching band, I heard a voice say "It's soft!" The voice sounded unashamedly delighted with itself, and completely surprised.

At Camp Betsey Cox, everything was done by the bell. Rising bell sounded at 7:30 A.M. to wake us up and set us on our sleepy way to washing up at the wash house. The breakfast bell rang at 8:00, right after we assembled to say the Pledge of Allegiance. The morning activities bell was at 9:30, the lunch bell at noon, and on and on throughout the day.

But in spite of all this bell-ringing, Camp Betsey Cox was surprisingly unregimented. The camp was started by a Christian Scientist who believed in the basic perfectability of mankind and in each person's ability to solve her problems by applying the right mental effort. The prevailing philosophy of the camp was that freedom and choice equals responsibility and growth. Within certain boundaries, we were allowed to create our own daily schedules. If we wanted to spend every day practicing archery, we could. If we wanted to play tennis or ride horses until we dropped, that was our prerogative.

I loved it all. I loved just walking up the hill at the back of camp and into the woods, cool and fresh-smelling and quiet, with even the sound of my own steps cushioned by the pine needles beneath my bare feet.

Among the most popular activities was woodcraft, which theoretically meant learning how to survive in the woods and practically speaking meant learning how to cook all kinds of food outdoors in preparation for our overnight hiking trips. We learned how to boil down sap for maple syrup, how to identify edible berries and roots, how to roast hot dogs in an outdoor pit. Gamilah loved woodcraft. She'd head straight to it after breakfast, cook and eat all morning, then go to lunch. After a few weeks at camp she'd get to the point where the buttons on her shorts were having trouble connecting.

Our only obligations at Camp Betsey Cox were to follow camp rules, take swimming lessons, and contribute to the community by taking our turns with certain camp jobs—setting the table for breakfast, sorting mail in the post office, weeding the vegetable patch. One year my job was to pick up and sort the mail. The sorting was great, but picking up the mail from what we called the Big House could be an exercise in terror. That was because the owners had a dog, a huge German shepherd named Notcha, and you never knew where he might lurk. One day my friends Lori, Kathy, and Lisa went with me to get the mail. But Notcha was tied up outside, and when we came near he began to bark. We were terrified. It took forever for us to work up the courage to dash past him and grab the mail. Once we did, we hauled ass out of there, giggling hysterically with fear.

Lisa Stroud was one of my best friends at camp, and she lived at our house, off and on, from the time she was seven or eight until she was about ten. I think Mommy, in her eternal generosity, must have thought raising seven girls could not be much harder than raising six, so when Miss Simone asked if Mommy could watch Lisa while she was on tour in Europe, Mommy said yes. It was great for me—Lisa and I were the same age and it was like having a twin. We called each other god-sisters. We played together, went to school together, danced to Miriam Makeba together, traveled to camp together. We shared my bedroom and took yoga classes together. She was a member of the family.

Sometimes Lisa and I played at her house under the care of her very young, very blonde housekeeper, in a backyard so verdant and lush it seemed more like a tropical jungle than a garden. The yard had one of those tire swings on which we would fly around and around and around, or else we'd shoot Silly String at each other, later getting into trouble because we were not supposed to let it stick to the outdoor furniture. And when Miss Simone came home she would sit at her great, black piano with a glass of wine and sing great, touching, soul-felt revolutionary songs like "To Be Young, Gifted and Black" in her amazing voice. And Lisa and I would sing along.

In the evenings at Camp Betsey Cox, the whole camp would walk over to Blueberry Field for vespers. We all sat in a big circle, looking out over the valley with the Green Mountains slowly disappearing as the sun went down. The counselors would try to lead us in earnest discussions about President Nixon or the Pentagon Papers or the war in Vietnam, but to most of us girls those things seemed as distant as the stars appearing in the sky above our heads. We just wanted to sit there in the gathering dusk, feeling all warm and sisterly, and sing "Kum Ba Yah" or "Country Road" while somebody strummed along on the guitar.

On Saturday nights we would have square dances or socials with the boys from neighboring Camp Sangamon.

Sometimes my mother would drive up to visit us during the middle of camp. It was always so exciting when she came. I remember once she brought us new dresses to wear to the square dances the counselors organized with the boys from Camp Sangamon. The dresses were ankle-length, with puffy sleeves and piping around the front and ruffles around the hem. Gamilah and I put them on and thought we were the most fashionable girls on the East Coast. My mother laughed and hugged us as we beamed. Then she put us in the car and drove us over to see Attallah and Qubilah at their camp, and the five of us spent the whole afternoon together. It was one of the best days of my young life.

But as much as I loved summer camp, I always missed my mother. Not being with her was the one sorrow in the otherwise idyllic world of Camp Betsey Cox. My mother was always the most important person in the world to me, and in times of stress or pain, I thought of no one else.

During my second summer at camp I was climbing a tree one day when I had an accident. It appeared a cat had been climbing the tree before me and had left behind a little present, into which I stepped and which made my foot slip so that I fell from the tree and landed on my arm. For one, long, unending moment I lay on the ground, silent and disbelieving, unable to even breathe. Then the pain came roaring in and I screamed. One of the girls with me shook herself from her stupor and went yelling for the camp nurse. Gamilah, who had also been climbing the tree but missed the cat poop, leapt down beside me and burst into tears. "Yasah! Yasah!" she sobbed, nearly as hysterical as I was. "Help! Help!" she yelled, but I couldn't hear her over my own screams.

The pain was excruciating, as though the earth, furious at my arrogance in trying to climb above it, had reached up and snatched me back down and snapped my arm in two, which in a way it had. I thought I was dying, and in that moment of fear I didn't think about my father and I didn't think about my sisters. The only person in my thoughts was my mother. "Tell Mommy I love her!" I cried to Gamilah. "Tell her she was the most important person in my life!"

I kept saying the same thing over and over, even as the counselors and staff arrived at the scene and scooped me off the ground. I said it even as they drove me into the town to the local hospital and as the doctors set my broken arm. "I'm dying," I said, a little less urgently once the painkillers kicked in. "Tell Mommy I love her. Tell her she was the last thing on my mind."

Mommy, though, had many other things besides me on her mind.

For one thing, there was the financial and emotional support of all of us. My mother had gone back to work part-time as a nurse, often working the late-evening or overnight shift so she could be home with us during the day. By this time she had received whatever modest sum she was going to get from the publication of *The Autobiography of Malcolm X*, and there was still the small circle of giving people around helping to make sure we survived. But the brunt of the responsibility for the six of us fell squarely on my mother. She did it all. "If I didn't make the money and bring the food in and pay the mortgage and pay the car note, and pay the school bill, we didn't eat, we didn't sleep, we didn't have a house," she wrote once. "I had to do everything."

There was also my mother's lingering grief. With my father's death, she had lost not just a husband but a friend and a lover, and eight years is not too much to grieve such a loss. It angers me when someone tries to portray my father as a sinister or, worse, a violent man. He was so far from that. My father was warm and personable and loving, and he poured all of that emotion out on my mother, whom he was crazy about.

Theirs was a great love story; not many people know that. Everyone who knew my parents as newlyweds tells me how tender, how sweet, and how romantic Malcolm was toward Mommy. During my mother's pregnancies, my father always made certain he was the one who took her to the doctor for her checkups. If he was going to be out of town on the day of the appointment, he would cancel it. After my oldest sister Attallah was born, my father, on those rare occasions when he was not traveling, sometimes took his family to the beach. "While he wrote his speeches," my mother wrote, "the baby and I would sit on the sand or play in the water. He used to read poetry to us, too, and was very good at it. He was also very complimentary in an offhanded kind of way. If I were to cook something especially good, he used to say, 'I can cook, you know, Betty. If necessary, I'll cook in a minute.' But he never cooked the entire time we were married."

Whenever my father traveled, which was often, he always made sure to telephone my mother and let her know where he was. And often during these conversations he would say, "Betty, go look in the kitchen cupboard" or "Go look under the pillow in our bedroom." My mother would do as he asked and find, tucked away, a love note or a ten-dollar bill he left for her to buy herself some special treat. He loved to make her laugh. He loved to compliment her on her beauty and her intelligence and her good cooking. She loved caring for him and learning from him and offering him the sustenance only she could provide. In his autobiography, my father said, "She's the only woman I ever even thought about loving. And she's one of the very few whom I have ever trusted." In an article for *Ebony*, my mother wrote, "In retrospect, marriage to Malcolm was hectic, beautiful and unforgettable—the greatest thing in my life."

So I have to believe that even as I was learning how to row a boat and build a fire in the woods, my mother was still struggling with her grief. She did so privately, keeping her pain hidden from the eyes of the world and from us.

And on top of all that, she was working through an issue that must have been, in some ways, much more difficult than any of the others. In the wake of my father's death, Mommy had begun taking the first few tentative steps in creating, or re-creating, her own identity, one that was proudly linked to, but distinct from, that of Malcolm X. She had begun the challenge of becoming more fully herself.

That's not to say Mommy was a wallflower who had to learn to stand on her own for the first time in her life. Betty Sanders possessed drive and ambition long before she met my father. She had already traveled from a comfortable, sheltered life in Detroit to racist Alabama and then to the bright lights of New York. She had already earned her nursing degree. And in marrying my father, she had, for the first time in her life, defied the wishes of her parents.

Even as a member of the Nation of Islam, which taught that women were to be subservient, my mother maintained her sense of independence. She was a nurse, she taught classes for Muslim women, and she developed curriculum at mosques up and down the East Coast. If someone asked her opinion, she gave it, wholeheartedly and without hesitation, not believing she should keep quiet just because she was a woman or the wife of Malcolm X. She declined to be a second-class citizen in the same way she declined to cover her hair. She believed hair covering was a cultural dictate not a religious one, and she chose not to follow it. Her sister-in-law, Dr. Ameenah Omar, said my mother refused to look anything but beautiful. She was beautiful and she wanted to look that way.

Nor did she ever, in her marriage to my father, take the backseat. My mother embraced her position as a wife, mother, and homemaker when she married my father, but she was not passive or submissive. She knew exactly who she was. During the early days of their marriage my mother wanted to put her nursing degree to good use by working part-time outside the home. At the time, my father was completely devoted to Elijah Muhammad, and he devoted all his time and energy toward building the Nation of Islam

83

without any thought toward personal gain. My mother supported his work but also wanted her young family to have a measure of financial stability. She believed that by working she could help put money aside for a home of their own.

But my father would not even entertain the idea. According to Nation of Islam teachings, the woman's place was at home, devoted to the care of her husband and children. My mother was so unhappy with his refusal that she walked out on him—not once, but three times. The first time, just after Attallah was born, she went to her cousin's house in Brooklyn. The second time, after Qubilah was born, she ran to her father and stepmother's house in Philadelphia. The third time, after I came along, she went back to Detroit. Each time she left she knew my father would find her and bring her home. And she was always happy when he did.

But as hard as it is to maintain one's sense of self as the wife of a great man, it's even harder to do so as the widow of a martyr. A wife's duty is to love, cherish, and support the man; a widow's duty is to safeguard the legacy. That is an enormous responsibility if a person takes it seriously, and Mommy did. She knew how important to African Americans and oppressed people everywhere—and how unfinished—was my father's work. She knew it could not be left to misinterpretation or allowed to vanish into the dustbin of history.

One of the many bits of wisdom my mother passed on to us was that everyone has a purpose in this life. God is not random; each of us is here for a reason. Our job is to recognize that reason, embrace it, and put all our strength and effort into achieving whatever purpose the Creator set out for us. "You're either part of the solution or you're part of the problem," my mother used to say, quoting Brother Huey Newton. I spent much of my late teenage and early adult years wondering about my own purpose on this earth, but I never had to wonder about those of my parents.

More than almost anyone else, Malcolm X brought about a change in African Americans, not just in our social and legal status but in the way we viewed ourselves. Malcolm X taught us that centuries of slavery and oppression had combined to make us believe the myth of inferiority, and to act accordingly. "We didn't land on Plymouth Rock," he said often. "Plymouth Rock landed on us." But my father sought to liberate African Americans from the crippling effects of that oppression and myth. He sought to connect us with the true greatness of our heritage. He sought to link our struggle to the struggle of oppressed people everywhere and to empower all people of color to liberate themselves.

My mother never spoke about her purpose directly, but it was also crystal clear. God put her on this earth to love and support her husband, to raise his six daughters, and to do continuous battle on behalf of poor and struggling people everywhere, whether it was poor women in China, hungry children in Africa, or disaffected people in America. Her purpose was also to ensure my father's contributions were correctly positioned in the great international struggle for human rights.

By the time I was six or seven my mother had begun securing my father's legacy. She attended several public memorial services held for him. She granted select interviews with magazines such as

Ebony and *Essence* to make sure his memory was kept alive and not distorted by either the government, which feared him, or the well-meaning but misguided groups that sought to manipulate his message for their own purposes.

"What you have to understand," she said once in a speech, "is conditions for the African diaspora have not changed appreciably. A lot of very narrow-minded people say 'by any means necessary' was a violent statement. I say anyone who says 'by any means necessary' is a violent statement is violent themselves, because it is a comprehensive statement. If you write a proposal, they want to know about options; they want to know about variances. 'By any means necessary' is not violent. It's comprehensive. It could be political, social, religious.

"Politics have always been violent. Slander is violent. The violence in a storm, uprooting trees—that's violence. My husband was not violent. He was born into a violent climate. His ancestors came over here from Africa at the bottom of slave ships. He didn't put himself there."

In 1972, Mommy oversaw and approved a documentary about Daddy's life directed by Marvin Worth and based on *The Autobiography of Malcolm X*, written by my father with Alex Haley. My mother's friends Frances and John Keefe told me a story about this time. It took place during a showing of the documentary to benefit the Westchester County Day Care Council, an organization that set standards and developed curriculum for day care centers in our part of New York. My mother served as president of the board of directors for several years in the early 1970s.

At the end of the film an emotional Mrs. Keefe made her way

up the aisle toward Mommy, who was standing near the door greeting people as they left. Seeing my mother there, knowing how much she had suffered, Mrs. Keefe could not keep the tears from streaming down her face.

An angry young African American woman scoffed at Mrs. Keefe's tears. "What are you crying for, honky?" she said with contempt. "You don't know anything about this."

Mrs. Keefe was horrified. She didn't know how to respond to such anger, so she just lowered her eyes and kept walking up the aisle, prepared to keep going straight out into the night. But when she reached my mother, Mommy looked straight into her eyes and smiled. Then she opened her arms.

"Well, the face of that woman behind me fell," Mrs. Keefe said, remembering the incident with a laugh. "Betty hugged me and thanked us for coming. She was so regal. She was wonderful."

But the woman who safeguards a legacy must be careful. Keeping the flame can become a full-time job, can slowly squeeze out all other aspects of selfhood until there is very little left. Lord knows it would have been easy for my mother to curl up and die after my father was killed, but that's not the kind of person she was. It would have been easy, too, for her to simply crawl inside her widowhood and stay there, to perform a kind of emotional suttee, throwing herself onto her husband's burning funeral pyre. It would have been easy for her to spend the rest of her life as Mrs. Malcolm X.

But great men marry great women. And great women know they must carry on despite heartbreak and tragedy, know they must carve out a new life not only for their children but for themselves.

Coretta Scott King did it by founding the King Center for Non-violent Social Change to educate future generations of civil rights activists. Jacqueline Kennedy did it by marrying one of the world's wealthiest men and using that wealth to carve out some measure of privacy and normalcy for her children in New York City.

My mother did it by going back to school.

CHAPTER FIVE

Mommy's Home

I must have been seven or eight years old when Mommy first went back to school. She already had a registered nursing degree from the Brooklyn State Hospital School of Nursing and was working hard to support us. But hospital hours are long and irregular; trying to schedule her work around our care was difficult and, as she said, the baby-sitting fees were adding up. Mommy decided that if she wanted to build a stable financial foundation for her family, while at the same time positioning herself to carry on the struggle in which she had always believed and for which her husband gave his life, she would have to find a new profession. Naturally enough, she chose education. She began taking classes at Jersey City State College on her way to earning a bachelor's degree in public health administration and a master's degree in early childhood education.

While my mother went to school, a small cadre of people took turns caring for us. Sometimes our friend and neighbor Mrs. Elise Sherrer would pitch in. Mrs. Sherrer was the foster mother of Jean Owensby, who was also like a sister to us. Jean was closest in age to Attallah and was always in our yard playing or we in hers.

Sometimes our aunt Ruth, who was really my mother's distant cousin, would come to our house to baby-sit, or take us to her home on Pacific Street in Brooklyn. Aunt Ruth had an oversized studio in Bedford-Stuyvesant, and we loved hanging out with the other children who lived in the neighborhood. Aunt Ruth's block was bigger, wider, and less intimate than ours, which only added to the excitement and feel of being in the city.

We never thought of ourselves as suburban girls, and no one on Pacific Street ever made us feel that way. Mommy didn't let us roam wild across New York, but she did let us take the train down to Grand Central and the subway out to Aunt Ruth's house if Aunt Ruth couldn't come for us, and so we didn't feel out of place walking along city streets. We were sure we could handle ourselves, and for the most part we did.

There was one time, though, when I got taken by a local con man. Mommy had brought the three oldest girls beautiful, 24-carat bracelets from St. Croix, and I, in my youthful exuberance, accepted an offer from a local jewelry store owner to "trade." The bracelet he gave me was twice the size in width of my flowered bracelet from Mommy. I raced back to Aunt Ruth's house to show off my prize.

"You did what?" Qubilah asked.

"I traded. Don't you think it's pretty?" I twirled the bracelet around my wrist for her inspection.

"Yasah, this is not gold," Qubilah said.

"Yes it is."

"Let me see." Qubilah took the bracelet from my wrist and scratched it with a coin. Then she held her finger up for my inspection. "Yasah, gold doesn't come off."

Qubilah marched me back to that store and demanded the man return my bracelet, which he did. This is one of the stories I think about when people ask me what it was like to grow up in a houseful of girls, because it illustrates the best part of having five sisters: someone always has your back.

We loved Aunt Ruth. She was not even five feet tall, with ample hips and arresting gray eyes. She spoiled us in some ways, buying us things Mommy did not buy. But Aunt Ruth did have her limits, and when we crossed them, she was old school. When Mommy wanted to physically discipline us, she would take one of the small, wooden paddles—the kind that came with a rubberband-like string and ball attached—and smack our hands a couple of times, relying more upon the pain of her disappointment than the pain of our bodies to make her point. (Still, she used the paddles. I think a lot of parents used that same method, which is probably why they stopped making those paddle balls. I imagine children all over the country standing in toy stores and shaking their heads, "No, that's okay, Mommy. I don't want another one of *those*.")

But Aunt Ruth wasn't interested in paddles; Aunt Ruth believed in the switch. To us, this was like something from plantation days. The idea of switches was so old-fashioned, so completely unlike our mother that I think the first time Aunt Ruth made clear her intentions we all just sat around, more stunned than afraid. *She's going to whip us with what?* Our house sat on a hill and you had to climb two sets of stairs to reach the front door; a walkway between the two sets of stairs was graced by a set of bushes. Whenever one of us did something really bad, Aunt Ruth would go out the door, down that long second set of stairs, and break off a piece of one of those bushes. Then, taking her time, she would climb back up, stripping the switch of its leaves as she came. I remember when we once stayed out past our curfew; Aunt Ruth came up the street to the top of the hill that entered into the woods, our playing grounds, at the end of Cedar Avenue, where we hung out with all the other neighborhood children, and spanked us all the way back to our house. My sisters and I tore down that hill, leaving in our wake a trail of laughter from our friends.

And then there were the housekeepers my mother hired. They, by and large, did not spank us, whether by direction from our mother or of their own restraint, and the result was that we pretty much ran roughshod over them. There were probably a half-dozen in all, but the two who remained with us the longest were Ms. Hopgood and Ms. Thomas.

Ms. Hopgood and Ms. Thomas were sweet, loving African American women, sisters, from the South. Both were probably in their late fifties or early sixties, though adults always seem older to children so I can't be sure. Ms. Hopgood was a full-figured woman, with beautiful thick gray hair that she wore long and pulled back into a braid. Ms. Thomas was more slender than her sister, with softer features and a softer disposition to match.

They both wore white uniform dresses whenever they were at our house, but Ms. Hopgood liked to snazz hers up by wearing a pretty pink apron on top. Ms. Thomas did most of the cooking; cupcakes were her specialty. Following Mommy's instructions, she would make them from healthy batters of wheat germ and whole-wheat flour and shredded carrots or mashed bananas and then frost them with fluffy pink icing that made our little stomachs jump with joy and our hands itchy with anticipation. But there was no sneaking early cupcakes with Ms. Thomas around. She could be nowhere in sight when I tiptoed into the kitchen and opened the refrigerator door, and just as my hand was reaching that pink treasure I would hear, "Get your hand off my cupcake!" I was always surprised and impressed; I thought Ms. Thomas must be some kind of special woman with the ability to see through walls. It never occurred to me that from her room next to the kitchen she could hear the refrigerator door open and guess the rest.

Ms. Hopgood took care of cleaning and managing the house. She was forever sweeping or mopping or dusting or picking up, trying to keep ahead of the household chaos that comes with six children. She would shoo us away from the kitchen after she had mopped. "Don't you girls track dirt onto my clean floor!" I always found what she said odd because I knew it wasn't *her* floor. The sisters Thomas and Hopgood were a possessive pair.

Of the two, Ms. Thomas was the more loving, the one more likely to grab a hug or dispense a quick kiss on the cheek. But they were both sweet, wonderful women who treated us as if we were their own. I don't know why we tortured them so, other than the fact that we were kids and they were not our mother.

Most of what we did was just the normal, house-wrecking stuff of high-spirited children at play. One time we were walking through the woods at the end of Cedar Avenue and came across a teenaged girl and boy kissing. We hounded that couple like they were criminals, chasing them through the woods and screaming at the tops of our lungs, "Kiss! Kiss! Woo, woo, woo!" We made a mess in the basement by playing around with the stacks of canned goods my mother kept for emergencies. We watched a "Little Rascals" episode where the rascals climbed a magic beanstalk into the sky and got chased by a giant, and it looked so exciting, so magical, that we immediately went down into the basement and grabbed one of my mother's silver, industrial-size cans of beans. We removed the top lid, grabbed a handful of beans and planted them all over the backyard. For weeks Gamilah, Qubilah, and I watched those beans, waiting for them to sprout overnight and grow into the sky. They never did.

We stumbled upon the cans my mother used to collect money for UNICEF and thought we'd discovered a secret treasure of our own. Malaak, Malikah, Gamilah, and I popped open the cans and shook the money all over the floor. Then we gathered it up and hiked miles into town to a local restaurant called Wesson's where we gorged ourselves on the greasy hamburgers, french fries, pickles, and ketchup our mother did not allow us to eat at home.

But sometimes our horseplay was directed straight at the housekeepers. One night my sisters Gamilah, Malaak, and I were upstairs in our bedroom, playing around when we should have been asleep. We had the television on and the chess- and checkerboards out. I was playing checkers with Malaak. She kept winning and laughing; I kept demanding a rematch because everyone knew she was much too young to beat me at anything.

Suddenly we heard Ms. Hopgood climbing the stairs and decided to play a little joke. We jumped into bed and pulled the covers over our heads. When she opened the door, we jumped out of bed and ran into our bathroom, pretending we had just woken up and thought it was morning. "Gotta get to school, gotta get to school!" we called as we ran around like maniacs, washing our faces and pulling clothes from our drawers.

Poor bewildered Ms. Hopgood didn't know what to do.

"Girls, girls, please!" she called from the doorway. "Please, get in bed! It's nine o'clock at night!" It's amazing we didn't give her a heart attack.

We were so high-spirited we actually drove one housekeeper away. Her name was Patricia, she was from Trinidad, and she was tall and tough and no-nonsense, a woman who'd had to make her own way in a difficult world. Still, for all her toughness, Patricia was at a complete loss as to how to rein us in. Whenever she took us out to eat at the local diner, we would all sit together in a booth, ignoring her and giggling and saying our names fast—AttallahQubilahIlyasahGamilahMalikahMalaak—to make people think we were speaking a foreign language. If we spoke to Patricia, we'd say her name very loudly because we didn't want anyone to think she was our mother. "*Patricia,* please pass the salt." "Can I have french fries, *Patricia?*" "Will you please pass the jelly, *Patricia?*"

The one thing about our house that gave Patricia pleasure was the colorful and beautiful hats my grandmother Sanders from Philadelphia wore whenever she came to visit. Patricia admired the hats so much and so often that my grandmother offered to send her one when she returned home to Philadelphia. Patricia was overjoyed with the idea. Every day she watched the mail, waiting for that hat.

But one day she must have finally gotten fed up. We were real terrors that day, bouncing off the walls, ignoring her pleas to do our homework, sit down during dinner, pick up our toys. That evening, Patricia casually asked Attallah when the last bus for New York City left town. Not thinking anything about it, Attallah told her it was some time around 11:00 P.M.

Patricia put us to bed early that night. The next morning, we got up and went downstairs to her room where she slept. The bed was empty and made. Patricia was gone. Later that afternoon the mailman arrived, bearing Patricia's hat.

After receiving her bachelor's and master's degrees from Jersey City State College, my mother decided to pursue her doctorate. Her friends were supportive, but even they wondered how in the world she would manage such a thing. How could a single mother of six even hope to find the long hours and uninterrupted time needed to write a doctoral thesis? But my mother was determined. Anything she put her mind to, she would accomplish.

My mother had been given the name of Dr. Norma Jean Anderson, a dean at the University of Massachusetts, who was known for her aggressive and successful efforts in bringing African American and Latino students into the undergraduate and graduate programs at UMass. It was Dr. Anderson who advised and guided both Bill Cosby and his wife, Camille Cosby, as they earned their doctorates. In fact, Bill Cosby was just finishing his doctoral program when my mother began hers.

When Mommy called Dr. Anderson she asked if the dean knew who she was. Dr. Anderson said she did.

Then Mommy told her, "What I really need is to come there. I think now is the time for me to go to school."

Dr. Anderson said, "Great. Come on."

I think my mother chose UMass not only because of Dr. Anderson, but because she thought that in the quiet, secluded college town of Amherst, far from the media frenzy of New York, far from the city her husband loved, she could find some peace. Her presence at UMass caused some buzz and drew some attention, but with Dr. Anderson's support my mother did not let it bother or distract her from the work at hand. In Norma Jean Anderson Mommy found not just a mentor but a dear friend. Sometimes when my mother drove to Amherst to attend classes, she would stay in a hotel. But many times she stayed at the home of Dr. Anderson and her husband, the Reverend LaVerne W. Anderson, a minister in the Church of God in Christ, and their three children. She and Dr. Anderson shared many lunches and long, long talks about child-rearing, spirituality, marriage, and love. "We'd talk," Dr. Anderson told me. "We'd talk about joyful things, the possibilities, the way to live life and live it gracefully."

For my mother, who craved people who would treat her as a human being, not as an icon, I'm sure the three-hour commute each way seemed like little enough in exchange.

Mommy arranged her schedule so that she would leave for Massachusetts on Sunday evening. Before leaving she would always take us to the mosque and some kind of cultural event, then come home and do our hair. That was her personal time with each of us, the time she spent washing, brushing, and lovingly braiding six heads. It would take her hours, of course, but she always took her time. "I want to make my baby pretty," she would say. Then she'd pack up and leave that evening, or sometimes early Monday morning, and make the drive up to Amherst in her blue Oldsmobile.

She would stay in Amherst until Wednesday, then return home to us.

My mother kept us from missing her too much by keeping us busy. We were on such a routine—Monday, charm school or drama class; Tuesday, music lessons; Wednesday, African history tutors— that the early part of the week always flew by, and before we knew it, it was Wednesday night and Mommy's blue car was pulling up the drive. "Mommy's home! Mommy's home!" we would call to one another excitedly. We were always so happy to see her, and she was happy to see us. We would fall into her arms and she, tired but energized by her mission and by us, would eagerly return the hugs. On Thursday night she'd take us all out to dinner where we would order chicken and vegetables and talk about the week just past. It was just a local diner, but my mother's regal presence made us think we were dining in the fanciest of restaurants.

Back home for four, short days, Mommy concentrated on giving each of us the attention we needed, on making sure the house was running smoothly, and on her coursework, which was substantial. Some days she had so many books and papers and pamphlets that she would move from her desk to the dining room floor, spreading her work around her like a quilt. She would spend hours like that, reading and making notes. Watching her study filled me with awe. Boy, college looked *hard*. In fact, it looked so hard I made up my ten-year-old mind not to go.

But I think my mother was deliberate about letting her girls see her work hard on her doctorate, because she wanted us to know that perseverance and doggedness would prevail in the end, despite any obstacles. And prevail they did for Mommy. In 1975, after three intense, hardworking years, Betty Shabazz was awarded her doctorate from the University of Massachusetts. She wrote her dissertation on the Organization of African Unity, especially the organization's educational component. The OAU is the organization after which my father was modeling his Organization of Afro-American Unity at the time of his death.

I was thirteen when Mommy received her Ph.D. from the University of Massachusetts. It was such an exciting time. She talked about it for weeks, and we all got new dresses for the occasion; the ones Gamilah and I wore were navy blue with light green piping across the shoulders and down the sleeve. We all piled into the car and drove up to Amherst with Mommy, seeing the campus for the first time. I thought the graceful buildings and lush green lawns were beautiful, like something out of a fairy tale. When they called my mother's name during the ceremony we all stood up and cheered our heads off. Mommy looked up at where we were sitting and waved. She made it feel as though the ceremony was our ceremony, too, as if we all were graduating, which, in a way, I suppose we were. We were graduating into a new life.

CHAPTER SIX

Played

My mother was a private and cautious woman; under the circumstances in which she found herself, that fact comes as no surprise. The late 1960s and early 1970s were a time of deep suspicion among activists involved in the black nationalism and civil rights movements. Many African Americans at the time (and before, and since) developed a healthy paranoia to keep themselves aware of the routine threats to themselves and their families. There's an old saying about suspicion among African Americans, quoted by Maya Angelou in *I Know Why the Caged Bird Sings*: "If you ask a Negro where he's been, he'll tell you where he's going."

Few people had more cause for that kind of caution than Mommy, who lived not in fear, because fear is the opposite of faith, but certainly in apprehension that the people responsible for my father's brutal assassination would one day attempt another venomous strike.

Friends of my mother have told me that Mommy knew, probably even before my father, what was happening to them during those first, turbulent days of separating from the Nation of Islam. My father had dedicated twelve years of his life to building the Nation, and build it he did, from a handful of followers to an organization that numbered, at its height, in the tens of thousands. The Nation did not make Malcolm X. Malcolm X made the Nation, and he did so at great personal sacrifice because he believed so deeply and so completely in Elijah Muhammad, and because he knew that for African Americans to truly overcome, they must first be liberated from the myth of their own self-hate and inferiority. Mr. Muhammad was trying to do just that. `

Still, my father idolized him. So complete was Daddy's faith that when he learned Mr. Muhammad had broken his own moral teachings and fathered four children out of wedlock by two of his secretaries, then tried to cover it up, Daddy was truly shattered. "I felt as though something in nature had failed, like the sun or the stars," my father wrote. "It was that incredible a phenomenon to me—something too stupendous to conceive." Even then he still could not believe that Mr. Muhammad and the top ministers of the Nation would turn on him the way they did.

But my mother saw how the other ministers lived, in nice homes and with nice cars, while my father rejected personal gain. She felt the jealousies and hostilities simmering as her husband became more and more famous, more and more dedicated, more and more certain of his mission, as he *became* the Nation of Islam. My mother was smart and intuitive. She knew even before the threats, the phone calls, the firebombing that almost took all of our lives. "No one believed him," my mother told reporters in February 1965 after identifying my father's body at the New York medical examiner's office. "They never took him seriously; even after the bombing of our home they said he did it himself!" She was helpless to stop the martyrdom of her husband, but she was determined to protect the rest of her family. From that day at the Audubon when she heard the shots and threw her body atop our own, my mother never stopped shielding her six little girls.

In 1966 three men, all African Americans and all members of the Nation of Islam, were convicted of my father's murder. One, Talmadge Hayer, was the man who was chased from the ballroom and shot in the leg by an armed member of my father's security force. Hayer, surrounded by an angry crowd that day, was rescued by two police officers who happened to be cruising past in a patrol car. Hayer confessed to the shooting, saying he and two other men— not the two convicted—had been hired to kill Malcolm X. He refused to say by whom. The Government!

My mother wasn't worried only about the followers of Elijah Muhammad. Although she believed in her heart that the group was responsible for my father's assassination, she knew there were other forces at work during those last, terrible months. Neither she nor my father believed the Nation could have been responsible for *all* the intimidation and *all* the threats made against my father's life. My father was a key architect of the training received by the Fruit of Islam, the security and self-defense arm of the Nation. He knew how they were taught to think, believe, and act. He knew what they could and could not do. Nor could the Nation have had my father declared "an undesirable person" by the French government and asked to leave the country a few weeks before his transition.

There's no question Malcolm X made the U.S. government very nervous. When my father traveled abroad in April 1964 he was greeted enthusiastically by world leaders and private citizens alike. Prince Faisal, the ruler of Saudi Arabia, granted my father an audience and made him a guest of the state. He addressed the parliament in Ghana and spoke at the prestigious Ibadan University in Nigeria. When he returned to Africa later that same year, my father met with President Gamal Abdel Nasser of Egypt, President Nnamdi Azikiwe of Nigeria, and President Julius Nyerere of Tanzania. By October 1964, Malcolm X had met with eleven heads of state. Here was a man, an African American man, being received like a world leader, yet he was not an elected official, not a representative of the American government, and, in fact, like all African Americans, was not afforded even basic human rights in America. The Johnson government could not have been pleased.

What's more, throughout his trip to Africa, my father decried the mad rush by multimillion-dollar American corporations to exploit Africa's mineral resources just when the continent's emerging democracies most needed their own wealth. Was that seen as a threat? He also gained the support of more than thirty heads of state in his bid to take the United States before the United Nations on an accusation of denial of human rights. Was America being censured by the world, like South Africa or Angola, an image the government would have enjoyed?

Then there was the persistent and malicious charge that my father was fomenting violence among African Americans. Nothing could have been farther from the truth. Never, not once, did

103

Malcolm X ever advocate violence for violence's sake. Never, not once, was he ever involved in a violent racial episode.

My father's message to African Americans was not violence, but self-respect, self-assurance, and, if necessary, self-defense. He did not believe in turning the other cheek, but insisted we as a people had as much right as anyone else to defend ourselves if attacked, whether by white people carrying lynching ropes or white sheriffs wielding fire hoses. He said, "It is a miracle that 22 million black people have not risen up against their oppressors—in which they would have been justified by all moral criteria, and even by the democratic tradition. It is a miracle that the American black people have remained a peaceful people, while catching all the centuries of hell they have caught here in white man's heaven." For this, the FBI branded him a threat to the American way of life.

In September 1960, Fidel Castro visited the United States. New York City officials set up a hotel room for him in downtown Manhattan, but Castro said he wanted to stay in Harlem and to meet with Malcolm X. For this the FBI labeled my father a communist, even though Daddy made it clear that communism was not a viable choice for members of the Nation of Islam because communism recognized no God. Still, the FBI homed in ever more on the Nation and, specifically, on my father. He was harassed, followed, and spied upon. Black agents were paid to infiltrate the Nation and report on my father's every move. His letters were intercepted, his telephones tapped, his speeches recorded, his movements watched. At least one agent tailed him to Africa, and when he was confronted by my father, railed about Malcolm X being "Anti-American, un-American, subversive, seditious and probably Communist." The FBI file on my father runs thousands of pages long.

With the government on one side, racist whites on the other, and the Nation of Islam on the third, my father knew he would not live to an old age. He said, "My father and most of his brothers died by violence—my father because of what he believed in. To come right down to it, if I take the kind of things in which I believe, then add to that the kind of temperament that I have, plus the one hundred percent dedication I have to whatever I believe in—these are ingredients which make it just about impossible for me to die of old age."

In those early years after my father's death, Mommy rarely left the house without some kind of male protective accompaniment. These were not paid bodyguards; these were friends and followers of my father who felt it was their duty to protect Malcolm's widow and children. I think my mother could not have kept some of them from watching out for us if she'd wanted to.

There's a photograph of my mother in a 1969 *Ebony*. She's attending a memorial service for my father held at Junior High 271 in Brooklyn, and she stands beneath a bright light, surrounded by young brothers in black leather jackets and black berets who look like Black Panthers, though they are not identified as such. What the caption says is this: "Widow is not affiliated with para-military group, did not request guard." In the picture, the young brothers all lean forward, listening attentively while my mother, looking down, says something with a faraway smile on her face.

My mother's good friends John and Fran Keefe told me that when Mommy arrived to speak at their Scarsdale church one day in the late 1960s, her car was accompanied by two cars—one in front, one in back—each carrying three solemn-faced African American men. They surrounded her as she climbed from her car, then escorted her inside the elegant structure. I imagine the sight of my mother walking down the aisle with all those serious brothers gave the good people of Scarsdale something to discuss over dinner that night.

As a child I never knew about the bodyguards. My only memory, a fragment, is of being at some large event and seeing a line of tall, handsome men all dressed in black and staring straight ahead, their faces set. They seemed so serious to me, too serious. I smiled and waved, even twirled around, trying to get them to smile. Nothing, not even a blink. I had the feeling I could have turned cartwheels across the floor and they would have paid not the slightest bit of attention. That's how focused they were. But when and where this moment took place, I have no idea.

My mother must have gone to great lengths to keep us from finding out and possibly being frightened by the presence of the bodyguards. Did she meet them outside the house? Did they wait for her at the end of our driveway? I do not know, but I believe my mother deliberately kept these men out of our sight so we would not grow up surrounded by fear. "You have to remember that the three oldest girls can recall three different times when someone tried to kill their father," she told a magazine interviewer in 1969. "I can't completely erase this from their minds, but I can stress the happy times and put their minds at ease." Amazingly enough, though, either my mother or the simple passage of time managed to do just that—erase from my mind those terrible memories of my father's life being threatened. I do not remember ever once being afraid for myself or my family as a child. Although I knew some bad men had "hurt" Daddy, it never occurred to me that those bad men would want to hurt us, too.

But there were hints, suggestions, little indications that we were not like other families. My mother was keenly private and reserved, more so than most adults I knew. She had friends, but she kept us sheltered from most people. She rarely took us along when she spoke in public. If one of our housekeepers was off that day and Aunt Ruth couldn't make it, my mother would take us to our grandmother's house in Philadelphia and leave us there.

She was very conscious of what she talked about on the telephone, even with her closest girlfriends. You might ask her a question, or take the conversation in one direction, and she would, without warning, switch midstream to a completely unrelated subject. And we also knew what was all right to say on the phone and what was not. If my mother was going away for some length of time, we did not discuss the trip. If one of us was in some kind of trouble at home or at school, we would not discuss it on the telephone. I never felt shadowed or threatened, just cautious. My friend Lisa Anthony and I even developed a code for discussing boys; if I said I'd had some Doublemint gum recently it meant I had kissed my latest beau. For some reason we had four different telephone lines, with one of those red buttons to put people on hold.

"We're living under surveillance," Mommy would say sometimes, warning us to behave. She was never more explicit than that, at least not with me, but I came to understand her words as meaning we should act conscientiously, honestly, and decently on all occasions. My sisters and I knew we should, by no means, engage in any bad behavior. Later, as an adolescent, I came to understand my mother's warning as meaning that any trouble I might get into as a teenager would surely be thrown up in my face later in life. In other words, in this country, especially for African Americans, anything you do can and will be used against you. Watch yourself.

The summer I was fifteen I decided to visit a friend in the neighborhood. Normally my sisters and I dressed fashionably but modestly—no hot pants or halter tops for us. But for some reason this day I decided to wear a cute little shorts and shirt combination I had bought for summer camp. At camp everyone wore shorts; it was no big deal.

I was walking down the street, thinking how cute I looked, when my mother pulled up beside me in her car. "Get in," she ordered. I climbed into the passenger seat, surprised at the serious tone of her voice.

"What do you think you're doing, walking around here dressed like that?" she asked.

"Dressed like what?"

"Those shorts are too revealing," she said.

"But I wear these at camp," I argued. "Everybody wears shorts at camp."

But my mother was not a woman to waste time arguing with her children. When she set a rule, that was that. "Do not let me see you wearing that outfit around here again," she said. "You have to dress like a young lady and be mindful of what you wear, say, and do. Your father would not condone this dressing."

Now, this might have been simply the worried warning of any mother concerned that her adolescent daughter's body was maturing faster than her sense of the world, and I probably took it that way. But part of me wonders now if she was not also trying to gently prepare me for the scrutiny that would come my way as the daughter of Malcolm X. Perhaps the reason she did not address the issue more forcefully with her daughters is that she did not want us to focus our lives on it, to allow what people said or thought of us to determine what we thought about ourselves. As I matured and thought anew about her advice to be careful in everything we said and did, I found this meaning: I had to be conscious of the decisions I made, and I had to make the right decisions—and "right" meant what was right in the eyes of God, not other people.

It's really the same thing I tell my nephew Malcolm: He must choose his own friends rather than allow people to choose him. You never know what ideas or passions or assumptions people will try to project on you, especially if you are the daughter or grandson of an icon. True friends will allow you to be you.

My mother was conscious of our security, but she was not paranoid and she did not raise us to be that way. She did not smother us with watchfulness or hover over us. She taught us not fear and suspicion but optimism. "Look for the good and praise it," she said over and over again. When we were at home, we were allowed to play outside, in the backyard, in the yards of friends, and even to roam the neighborhood just like any other children. It was my grandparents, and not my mother, who raised my anger by being what I thought was vastly overprotective.

After camp every summer my sisters and I went to spend a few weeks at my grandfather's house in Philadelphia. Shelman Sanders—we called him JuJu—was my mother's biological father, and his wife, Madeline, was my mother's stepmother. They had three grown sons: Uncle Shelman Jr., whom we called Uncle Dickey; Uncle Stanley; and Uncle John.

My grandparents weren't worried about the Nation of Islam or the federal government; these were vague and distant threats. They were worried about the normal, everyday dangers that can befall a young girl in the city—accidents, illicit substances, crime, and, most of all, boys. Their way of keeping us safe and secure was simple: We were never allowed out without an adult. My grandparents took us lots of places—to church, to the park for picnics, even to the zoo. But if we were home at their house we could venture no farther than the front steps alone. We couldn't step into the street to join a kickball game. We couldn't visit the homes of other children or run around the corner to the store for a bag of potato chips. If one of my uncles was going to the store for a package of gum, we'd cluster around him, begging "Please, can we go?" because the only time we could leave that block was escorted by an uncle or in a family member's car.

There was a boy in the neighborhood named Donald Bird. He was a fine brother with Ethiopian muscles and beautiful Sudanese skin. We liked each other, and if he saw me sitting on the steps of my grandparents' house he would come over to talk, at least until one of my uncles sauntered outside, leaned against the railing, and gave Donald "The Stare." But that didn't stop me from giving Donald my address in Mount Vernon. We exchanged a few letters during the school year, and as the summer of my fifteenth birthday rolled around, we arranged to meet one day away from the prying eyes of my family.

I arranged to spend the day at the West Philadelphia home of

Uncle Dickey, because one of Donald's brothers had a house in the same neighborhood. I waited until Uncle Dickey was out of the house, then asked his wife, Aunt Pat, if I could go to the store. Aunt Pat was a nurse, a calm and unflappable woman who seemed less worried about the lurking dangers of the streets.

"Sure," she said, not looking up from her newspaper. "Don't take too long."

I flew out of the house, giddy with freedom, and raced to the store where Don was waiting. He was dressed up pretty suave and even smelled good. Taking my hand, he smiled his movie-star smile. "Let's go to the mall," he said.

This was a great adventure for me—remember, I was fifteen years old but had almost never been anywhere, except the homes of a few girlfriends, without some member of my family along.

Don suggested we go over to the local shopping center and walk around. He bought me a soda and a soft pretzel and we held hands as we window-shopped. It was a lovely date. After a few hours we made our way back to the neighborhood and strolled over to Robin Hood Dell park, which was just across the street from my uncle Dickey's house. Don led me to one of the cozy gazebos that dot the park and we settled in there, talking and laughing, brushing hands, and, occasionally, lips. Don was so handsome and so sweet, so gently attentive; being with him put me in a blissful daze. I might have remained in that gazebo all day if I had not happened to glance across at my uncle's house and notice all the car lights out front. A lot of car lights on a lot of cars.

My heart leapt and I leapt with it. "I'd better get back," I said to Don.

He started walking me back to the house, but as we got closer I noticed that among the cars was one belonging to my grandfather. Then Uncle John and Uncle Dickey appeared suddenly on the porch. They were talking low and seriously to each other and looking very agitated. The sight of them stopped me in my tracks.

"You better go," I said.

"Why? What's wrong?" Don said. He was trying to be cool, but I could hear the tremble in his voice. My uncles were big men.

"They're mad," I said. "You better go."

"Well, if you're sure," Don said, already backing away.

"I'm sure. I'll call you. Go on."

Don turned and started walking away just as my uncle Dickey spotted me. He called to my grandfather, who was still inside, then waited. My grandfather came through the screen door like an explosion. He was a big man, very stocky and strong. He looked like Duke Ellington if Duke Ellington was highly agitated, and he crossed the porch and went down the steps like Mike Tyson without even breaking stride. I stood on that hot Philadelphia sidewalk watching him come storming toward me like the Jolly Green Giant. Except his face was not jolly at all. He was hotly furious.

My heart racing, I scrambled to prepare my defense. *I didn't do anything wrong. Aunt Pat said I could go to the store and I went to the store and I am fifteen anyway, not a child, what is the problem?*

But my grandfather did not give me a chance to excuse myself. He walked straight up to me and slapped me in the face.

The rest of the afternoon is a blur of pain and shock and tears and angry shouts. Somehow I got back in the house, where my grandparents and uncles all berated me for running off with some boy and disappearing like that. Didn't I know how dangerous that was? Didn't I know what terrible crimes could have befallen me?

Mommy, Attallah, Daddy holding Qubilah, and Muhammad Ali with me on his lap. *(Photo copyright Robert L. Haggins. Reprinted with permission.)*

Attallah, Ilyasah, and Qubilah in our backyard. Mommy couldn't get those scarves and dresses on me. . . . I probably would have snatched them off. *(Photo copyright Robert L. Haggins. Reprinted with permission.)*

That's me with my head on Attallah's lap. *(Photo copyright Robert L. Haggins. Reprinted with permission.)*

On the front steps of our house in 1964. *Left to right:* Qubilah, Attallah, me, and Gamilah in Mommy's arm. *(Photo copyright Robert L. Haggins. Reprinted with permission.)*

Me, Daddy, and Qubilah. *(Photo copyright Robert L. Haggins. Reprinted with permission.)*

Mommy looking at a photo
of Daddy in 1965.
(Photo courtesy of the author)

Mommy and the twins in 1968. They were
in her belly when daddy was assassinated.
*(Photo copyright Merrill A. Roberts Jr. Reprinted
with permission.)*

My uncles, Wesley and Wilfred,
thirty-three years after their
brother was assassinated.
(Photo courtesy of the author)

At one of Daddy's memorial services. *Left to right, top:* Qubilah and Attallah; *bottom:* Malikah, Ilyasah, Mommy, Gamilah, and Malaak. *(Photo copyright Merrill A. Roberts Jr. Reprinted with permission.)*

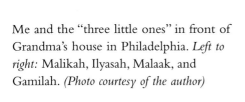

Lisa Anthony! Lisa (John Anthony's daughter) and I were inseparable as far back as the early seventies. *(Photo courtesy of the author)*

My childhood father figure: Mr. John Arthur.
(Photo courtesy of the author)

Me and the "three little ones" in front of Grandma's house in Philadelphia. *Left to right:* Malikah, Ilyasah, Malaak, and Gamilah. *(Photo courtesy of the author)*

Making cookies at Camp Betsey Cox in July 1970. *(Photo courtesy of the author)*

The dreadful corn weeding at Camp Betsey Cox, July 1972. *(Photo courtesy of the author)*

Ninth grade at the Masters School. *(Photo copyright West End Entertainment. Reprinted with permission.)*

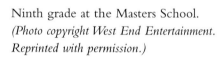

Me and some of my soul sisters at the Masters School. *(Photo copyright West End Entertainment. Reprinted with permission.)*

Me and my Hustling King, Michael Peeples. . . . I think we still have the dance routine down. *(Photo courtesy of the author)*

Malaak and me in 1986. *(Photo courtesy of the author)*

My days as an aspiring model. I thought I had *it*, but the agencies thought otherwise. . . . *(Photo courtesy of the author)*

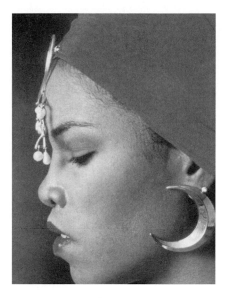

Me in my modeling days . . .
wishing I was queen of the Nile.
(Photo courtesy of the author)

One of my best friends, Crystal Christmas, and
me chilling at the airport. *(Photo courtesy of
the author)*

Jerrod and me. This is when my
5'11" frame could wear the highest
pair of heels because he was 6'11".
(Photo courtesy of the author)

Left to right: LaVallis, Susan Taylor, and Ilyasah. *(Photo courtesy of the author)*

Bernice King and me at one of
her dad's birthday celebrations.
(Photo courtesy of the author)

Terrie Williams, my spiritual sister, and me.
(Photo courtesy of the author)

Me and President Bill Clinton in South Africa.
(Photo courtesy of the author)

A profound experience
for me was reading the
biography of Winnie
Mandela . . . mind-blowing!
And so it was a most endearing
and heartfelt moment when
Gamilah and I met her.
(Photo courtesy of the author)

I spotted the Big Man, Shaquille, at Georgia's
in Cali, and he was kind enough to take
a photo with me. *(Photo courtesy of the author)*

Left to right, top: Deb and Liz; *bottom:* Ilyasah and Sooze. The Pendulum Gyrlz taking a peaceful moment. *(Photo courtesy of the author)*

Malikah, Auntie Mary Redd (Mommy's best friend), and me at a birthday party in 1998. *(Photo courtesy of the author)*

Malaak, Attallah, and me. *(Photo courtesy of the author)*

Me and Auntie Coretta.
(Photo courtesy of the author)

Gamilah, Malaak, Attallah, Qubilah, Ilyasah, and Malikah holding her baby girl.
(Photo courtesy Hakim Mutlaq © 2001. All Rights Reserved.)

My nephew Malcolm with his infamous smile.
(Photo courtesy of the author)

Malcolm and Mommy. *(Photo courtesy of the author)*

Didn't I know how worried my mother would have been had she known? Didn't I think about anyone but myself?

I was hurt and flabbergasted and angry myself. It was the first time in my life any man had ever hit me, and I was staggered by the injustice of it all. Why were they in such an uproar? What could I have possibly done to excuse my grandfather striking me like that? "What's the big deal? What's the big deal?" I kept asking, but no one answered me, at least not in a way that I could understand. I felt completely wronged. I locked myself in one of the bedrooms and wrote my mother a letter, begging her to let me come home. I couldn't understand how my grandmother could be so nice in some ways, taking us on picnics, letting us have potato chips and other goodies we weren't allowed at home, and in other ways be so incredibly mean.

"I don't know what's wrong with Grandma," I wrote. "She doesn't let us go out. She doesn't let us mingle with other people. She acts like we're too good for them. She just doesn't want young people to have any fun."

A week later, when my mother wrote back, it was to say something diplomatic like "When you're at your grandmother's house, you have to live by her rules." This, of course, was completely unsatisfactory to me. I could not understand how my mother could expect me to tolerate such behavior. I thought my grandparents and my uncles were paranoid and overprotective and crazy. I thought they were all very, very mean.

Looking back on it now, I understand how terrified my grandparents and uncles must have been that day. They knew the ways of the world, and they knew how unsuspecting and even innocent I still was. Against all odds my mother had raised us to believe the world was good, people were basically kind, African American brothers and sisters especially could be trusted to do no harm. So deeply embedded were these beliefs that even when one of the things my grandparents probably feared did happen to me, my brain would not fully comprehend it. I would subconsciously submerge the event and its effect upon me, rather than allow it to change the person I was.

I could probably count on one hand the number of times in my life I heard my mother speak the name Louis Farrakhan. And I wouldn't need even that hand to count the number of times she mentioned him when we were children because that number is zero. She never mentioned him. Not at all.

As I got older and the facts of my father's death trickled into my consciousness, I became aware of Mr. Farrakhan. I knew that whatever the truth about my father's death, there was something about Mr. Farrakhan I did not want to associate with. But I also knew that people aren't the final judges of other human beings, God is. So I never entertained negative thoughts about him, never wished him ill. And I never had any fear that whoever was responsible for my father's death would try to hurt me. I believe our lives on this earth are in greater hands than our own. However you're going to go, that's up to God.

What did upset me about Minister Farrakhan was his refusal to acknowledge all that Malcolm X did for the Nation. I once saw the minister on the "Arsenio Hall Show." When Arsenio asked him about Malcolm X, he said we were the only group of people who honor the dead; yet he kept referring to the Honorable Elijah Muhammad. He spoke eloquently of the Nation's efforts to help

African Americans, but made no mention of the fact that it was Daddy who most successfully organized those efforts, Daddy who organized temple after temple and brought thousands of new members to the fold. It was my father who incorporated Garveyism into the Nation's philosophy and my father who encouraged the Nation to cease essentially withdrawing from the black struggle and to become a force in America's political and social life. It was my father who created *Muhammad Speaks*, the Nation's newspaper. It was my father who mentored other young leaders of the Nation, including Minister Farrakhan.

When I see Minister Farrakhan talking about Marcus Garvey, teaching about the international brotherhood shared by people of African descent worldwide, informing people of international views on ancient cultures, I know he is following in the footsteps of my father. In a way, I enjoy hearing him speak because I know he is the only person addressing and informing us of those topics today. Obviously he admired my father, because he studied him. But for him not to acknowledge that debt bothers me the most.

In 1995 my mother attended the Million Man March in Washington. She went not because of Minister Farrakhan but because of the stated goal of the march—men uniting in pride and commitment to their families, their communities, and their self-respect.

At the Million Man March, Mommy was embraced by dozens upon dozens of sisters of the Nation of Islam, some of whom had once been like true sisters to her but to whom she had not spoken in many years. Watching all those sisters hover around my mother made me both happy and sad. I saw the sense of comfort, the ease that existed among these women when history and pain and torn allegiances were finally pushed aside. Being back among the members of the Nation must have been difficult for my mother, and putting myself in her place, I was nearly overwhelmed. It broke my heart to look at all those beautiful African American sisters (and, for the first time in my life, Minister Farrakhan) and realize how our people were simply not strong enough back then to look at the bigger picture of what my father was about. Here you have someone who took on our entire struggle as a people, who sacrificed himself to liberate all Africans, in America and beyond. Yet African Americans allowed themselves to be part of his death, whether they helped to conspire against him or actually pulled the trigger. African Americans turned their backs on him and his wife, whether they denied the danger or refused to allow the use of a church for his funeral service. And African Americans allowed themselves to be part of the attempted murder of his crusade to free us all.

If you ask me, we, as a people, allowed ourselves to be played.

CHAPTER SEVEN

Hustle Queen

As a child, I often dreamt of my father. Sometimes these were flickering images: his face, his smile, his hand passing me an oatmeal cookie. Other times the dreams were long and complex, whole movies of my father in my mind. When I was ten I dreamt I walked out the back door of our house, down the stairs, past the grapevines, into the yard, and saw him sitting on the patio with the awning overhead and trees on the side. He sat in a huge chair, one that gleamed and glistened like a throne. I was so excited to see him, so happy I could not contain myself. "Daddy! Daddy!" I yelled, running toward him. He grinned that beautiful, full-face grin the world seldom saw but which those who knew my father basked in. Suddenly, he opened his arms wide. "Daddy!" I ran and ran and ran, but I could never get close enough to touch him. As soon as I did, something would happen and I would find myself back on those stairs again.

Months later I told my best friends Lisa Anthony and Kim Brown about the dream. We were having a sleepover at Lisa's house, a very special occasion because my mother did not allow us to spend the night at the home of anyone but relatives. But this time Mommy was in Africa and Aunt Ruth was in charge; for all her old-world disciplinary habits, Aunt Ruth was a pushover in certain areas. She bought the three little ones and me our first, unauthorized pairs of platform shoes from Abraham & Straus. And she let me sleep over at Lisa's house.

Lisa and I became fast friends on the first day of school at St. Joseph Montessori. She was beautiful, a golden, sun-kissed girl with big, doll eyes and thick black eyelashes. Her gorgeous black hair was so long and so thick she could pull it into a bun on top of her head and leave it that way for a week, brushing only the outside before going out each day. She lived in a huge house in New Rochelle with her father, who was from St. Kitts and owned his own business; her mother, who taught school; and her three sisters. I thought they were the perfect family, and they treated me like another daughter.

It was the Anthonys who stepped in one time when I was thirteen and Qubilah and I were feuding furiously. Like many closely spaced siblings, Qubilah and I were both the best of friends and the fiercest of enemies. As a child she tended to blame me for anything that wasn't good in her life, perhaps because I came along when she was only nineteen months old and gobbled up attention in the ways that babies do. She loved me and if anyone outside the family tried to hurt me Qubilah was there as my protector, but inside the house she tortured me. I don't even remember what set her off on that particular occasion, but she chased me through the house yelling "I'm going to get you!" And believe me, I was scared. Mother was away with the twins and it was just the three of us older girls at home. Attallah distanced herself from the fight, leaving me on my own.

Qubilah chased me through the hallway and through the dining room. Petrified, I managed to slip into the breakfast nook, close the door, and then slide into the closet, grabbing the telephone as I went. I called Lisa.

"Lisa!" I cried into the phone. "Help! Qubilah's going to get me! She's yelling and chasing me!"

Lisa ran to her father, who got into his car and drove to our house immediately. "Come with me, Ilyasah," he said. When Mommy returned Mr. Anthony called and offered to let me remain at their house for a week or so, until tempers cooled. Looking back now I see how remarkable a man he was, not only for opening his home to his daughter's friend, but for taking the tensions between two sisters seriously.

I loved sleeping over at Lisa's house. That night we did the usual things: ate popcorn and danced to music and giggled about boys. Then we all climbed into the bottom bunk bed in Lisa's room and talked about our dreams. When Kim heard mine she burst into tears.

"If you had actually gotten into your father's arms," she said, "you would have died in your sleep."

Now that was a frightening thought, one that would never have occurred to me. But Kim was a very spiritual person; she went to church all the time with her devoutly Baptist parents. I thought if anyone was capable of interpreting dreams, it would be her.

"Wow!" I said. And then, because Kim was crying, Lisa and I also burst into tears at the thought of me dying in my sleep to be with my father. We cried for maybe five full minutes, then wiped our tears and snuck downstairs to raid the kitchen in search of strawberry Pop-Tarts.

Mr. Anthony was the one adult who spoke to me directly about my father, the man. As I've said before, my mother did a superhuman job of keeping Daddy alive for us as a parent. But for all the times she referred to him in the present tense, for all the times she admonished us in his name—"You know Daddy would not like that!"—she rarely spoke about Malcolm X. I didn't learn about my father at home; I had to get older and read about him and ask my mother direct questions before she and I finally sat down to discuss his accomplishments and contributions. As a child, I knew my father was Malcolm X, and I knew Malcolm X had done something important for black people, something tremendously important. But what precisely that was, I did not know. My mother did not discuss his role in the human rights movement just as she did not discuss his death. Neither did Aunt Ruth or my uncles or my grandparents. Everyone was far too busy feeding and educating and protecting us—nourishing us—to focus on that.

But sometimes when I was visiting the Anthony house, Mr. Anthony would sit me down. "Ilyasah," he would say, "I loved your father. Your father was a powerful man, a great man, and a hero. I want you to know that."

Mr. Anthony would talk politics with me, discussing the plight of the African diaspora, the civil rights movement, affirmative action, and on and on and on. Most times I had no idea what he was talking about, but he spoke with such authority I strove to understand. I loved Mr. Anthony and I loved listening to him. He reminded me of Daddy: tall, handsome, commanding, and passionate about the predicament of African people and the human race. And I admired his total dedication to his wife and children.

He guided his children with firmness and love and sometimes with gentle good humor. As Lisa and I got older and began going out with friends or staying awake late on the weekends, Mr. Anthony began a habit of waking us up at the crack of dawn to make breakfast. The later we stayed out, or even just awake, the earlier he woke us to make a pot of tea or cook up enough pancakes or cheese blintzes to feed an army. We would stumble around the kitchen until finally we were awake enough to laugh about what he was doing to us.

But as much as I loved Mr. Anthony, being around him was sometimes painful. Watching him at the breakfast table, hearing him joke with his family, seeing him build, with his own hands, a gymnasium for his daughter—all of these things made me miss the father my mother had not been able to supply: the physical man. The presence of Mr. Anthony made real my father's absence.

Still, looking at Mr. Anthony, I also knew that if my father were alive, that was the kind of man he would be. And I knew the love I felt in the Anthony house was the kind of love I would feel if my father had not been taken from us. There was nothing the Anthonys didn't have, nothing that mattered. They were full of love, and they generously shared that love with me.

That I missed my father, even if subconsciously, was made evident by the way I sometimes reacted to tall, intelligent-looking black men. Once, when I was about thirteen or fourteen, I was taking the bus home from White Plains when I met a man who looked like Daddy. I started a conversation. He was about ten years older than myself, tall and dignified. He told me people often remarked on how much he resembled "Brother Malcolm." So naturally, I invited him home to meet Mommy.

When my mother walked into the house we were sitting in the breakfast nook having a snack. I'm sure she must have nearly fainted at the idea of her young daughter bringing strangers into the house. Fortunately the guy turned out to be harmless. He was one of those back-to-basics spiritual brothers who worshiped Malcolm's ideology and was thrilled to meet his family.

We had only sporadic contact with Daddy's family when we were young. I'm not sure of all the reasons, but I believe part of it was that my mother naturally turned to her own family in a time of such great need. Then, too, most of my father's brothers were at one time actively involved in the Nation; in fact, it was my uncles who introduced Daddy to the organization. When Daddy split with Elijah Muhammad, several of my uncles remained with the Nation and thus were forbidden contact with us. Right after Daddy was killed, my uncle Philbert was ordered by Nation officials to attend a press conference. When he arrived and sat on the stage, he was handed a statement condemning my father and ordered to read it, and so he did. On the Friday before Daddy was buried, both Uncle Wilfred and Uncle Philbert stood before thousands of Nation of Islam members in Chicago and urged unity with Elijah Muhammad.

Two other of my father's brothers, Wesley and Reginald, virtually disappeared after Daddy was assassinated, losing touch not only with us but with their other brothers and sisters. Uncle Wesley didn't show up until my mother's funeral.

But my mother never spoke ill of my father's family. What I

knew about the Littles I knew from my father's autobiography and, as I've said, that portrait was not completely accurate. As an adult I learned that some of my father's sisters and brothers were displeased with the way he portrayed the family in that book.

But even during those early, difficult years there was the occasional reaching-out from my father's family. Aunt Hilda, my father's eldest sister, sent us gift-wrapped mother-of-pearl necklaces and earrings. It was like receiving Nefertiti's treasure from the waters of the Nile, a grand and beautiful prize given by Daddy's sister, a real live blood relative. I was ecstatic.

When I was about ten, Uncle Wilfred came to visit us. I don't know the reason or the impetus; one day he was simply there and we were thrilled. He played with us, took us out to dinner, sat in our living room, and talked to us as if we were the most interesting people on earth. I was a happy child—Mommy worked so hard to see to that—but during those days of Uncle Wilfred's visit I felt a sense of peace and family togetherness that was above and beyond even our usual state. Looking back now I see that my uncle's presence filled a void I didn't realize existed. In him I saw my father and felt my father's love, and when Uncle Wilfred announced it was time for him to go I was devastated. How could he leave us? How could he be so mean?

I sobbed uncontrollably all the way to the airport and I sobbed as he waved and then disappeared onto the plane. No one could comfort me, not my sisters, not even Mommy. I could not understand why he was leaving us. I couldn't understand that he had a family and a home and responsibilities elsewhere, and even if I had understood, I probably would not have cared. He was my uncle, I loved him, and I wanted him to stay. He belonged with us.

Despite my teacher's shortcomings in African history, I enjoyed St. Joseph Montessori School. I loved the huge, open classrooms, the way younger children and older children intermingled and learned from one another (just like at home). I liked Mr. Schneider, who was six-foot-five, dark-haired, and from Switzerland, and who taught us geography and math in a booming German accent. "Sixteen times twenty-five divided by eight multiplied by three! Go!" he would bark as we sat around a long table, pencils in hand. If a student failed to follow instructions or lapsed in his work, Mr. Schneider would train his piercing eyes on the student's face and say, "You will regret!" He made regret sound like the worst thing that could happen to a person, like a slow, wasting disease that would haunt you the rest of your life. I vowed early on to view everything that happened to me in life and everything I did as a learning experience. I wanted never to regret anything.

I admired, if not exactly loved, our principal, Miss Ellis. She was a pretty, well-traveled, and impeccably put together Caribbean woman who ran the school like a drill sergeant. She issued commands and expected results. If you did something so awful as to warrant a trip to Miss Ellis, heaven help you. We feared Miss Ellis. She was so intimidating that students would begin crying and hiccuping even before they got to her office.

None of the teachers at St. Joseph's ever said anything to me about my father. If they knew who he was, and I'm sure they did since Attallah had attended the school before me, they kept their opinions about him to themselves.

But some of the children knew—or rather their parents knew. And not everyone was happy about it. There was a girl at

124

St. Joseph's named Claudine. Her mother was from Trinidad and her father from Switzerland and she was smart and funny and sweet and, like me, loved to dance. We hit it off immediately and became good friends. Claudine's mother was an intelligent and very strict woman who did not approve of Malcolm X and what she *thought* was his message. I don't know how I knew this—she never said anything to me directly—but I did.

One year Mommy went to a leather goods warehouse and bought a stack of purses for my sisters and me to give to our friends as Christmas presents. I picked the best of the bunch for Claudine, who accepted the gift with a squeal and a hug. But the next time I saw her, she gave the purse back.

"I'm sorry," she said. "My mother will not let me accept it."

"Why not?"

Poor Claudine looked as baffled as I felt. "You know. Because of your father."

I probably went home and asked Mommy, who treated the incident lightly and said something warm and distracting like "Well, precious, some people are just confused," and then sent me on my way. That was the way Mommy handled things and it worked pretty well; I don't remember being unduly upset by the incident and Claudine and I remained good friends (and are to this day). But I'm sure somewhere deep inside it had to hurt. My ten-year-old mind had to wonder why someone's mother did not want me giving her gifts. *What did Daddy ever do to her?*

I remember only one similar incident when the media-distorted image of my father directly affected my little world. There was a girl in my neighborhood named Renee. One day she told me flat out that her mother didn't want her playing with me because my

father was Malcolm X and therefore I must, in some way, be "bad."
One day not long afterward I happened to run into Renee's mother
on the street. "I never liked your father," she said. Her eyes were
wet and she was walking funny and her breath smelled strangely
sweet and so I just walked around her and went on home. I tried to
dismiss her comments; everyone knew Renee's mother was an al-
coholic, anyway. But in a way that just made it hurt more. How
could someone with a drinking problem think she was better than
my father? How could she think she was better than me?

I loved all the friends I made at St. Joseph's: Kim and Sybil and
Yvette and Carla and Monique and Claudine and Lisa. At the end
of each school year we would get together and perform a dance
number for the other students at the school, sometimes joined by a
girl named Robin Givens. Robin was as pretty then as she is now,
and everything she wore fit as if it had been hand-tailored just for
her, which maybe it was. She was always perfectly coifed, even
when we were practicing our dance routines. And practice we did,
for weeks ahead of time in one another's basements. I usually choreo-
graphed, taking various steps I had learned from my lessons in
African dance and modern dance and combining them with whatever moves I saw on "Soul Train" that week: the penguin or the
funky chicken mixed together with copious glides and splits. Whatever we saw the Jackson Five or the Spinners or the Temptations
doing is what we did while singing along to "Stop, the Love You
Save" or "Papa Was a Rolling Stone."

For all those reasons, graduation from St. Joseph's was very emotional for me. I was thirteen years old, poised at the threshold of
adulthood but not quite sure I really wanted to step into that room.

My friends and I would all be going to different high schools in the fall, and although we would still see one another, it would not be the same. Graduation was the breaking up of our family, the end of my being the mother hen to all my friends, the end of our childhood. We were moving on.

My mother helped eased the pain by letting me buy platform shoes for the graduation ceremony. All my friends had been strutting around in platforms for years, but Mommy did not believe in fads. She bought us Hush Puppies, Stride Rites, oxfords: sturdy, sensible, boring shoes. Some of the shoes she bought us were so tough we could have worked construction in them. But in honor of my maturing sensibilities, Mommy took me shopping and let me pick out a snazzy pair of camel-colored platform sandals and a gorgeous, camel-colored pantsuit. My mother always wore suits and so, standing in that dressing room mirror, looking at myself, I felt more like her, so grown-up and mature. I was sharp.

I wore that suit and my new platforms to graduation with pride, and performed, along with my friends, a final dance tribute to St. Joseph's to the tune "Maybe Tomorrow." We danced and raised our voices along with Michael Jackson's as tears streamed down our faces. It was kind of pathetic. Afterward Mommy gave me my graduation presents: a new watch, a new pocketbook, and a wallet to match. The wallet especially was exciting; after years of just tossing my money into my purse any old way, I could now place my dollar bills neatly in one compartment and my change in another. I felt so grown and organized. Mommy always told me I had to treat my money with respect.

In celebration, Mommy took me and a group of friends to the Embassy Diner, a favorite hangout of ours because the french fries were delicious and all the booths had little jukeboxes right there on the tables. We pooled our quarters and played Michael Jackson songs again and again, dancing near our table until Kitty the waitress came rushing up and told us to sit down.

Attallah and Qubilah were attending the United Nations International School in Manhattan, but that fall I enrolled in the Masters School, a private and, at the time, all-girls school in Dobbs Ferry. At the interview my mother sat up proud and straight and beautiful and answered every question the admissions staff threw my way. Finally one of them said, very kindly, "Well, Dr. Shabazz, can she speak?" But I couldn't, not really. I managed to squeak out enough intelligible words to get me admitted, but they had seen the reality of my life. My mother always spoke for me, just as she did for my sisters. My mother did everything for us, bless her heart.

Walking onto the Masters campus for the first time I felt as though I had fallen into the pages of some English novel. The grounds were immaculately manicured, the buildings stately and stone, the view over the Hudson River magnificent. The girls were shiny and beautiful and sophisticated; they had perfect posture and smoked cigarettes in the rec room and talked casually about sex. Everything about the Masters School was beautiful and everything exuded wealth.

I entered Masters—or Dobbs, as we called it—as a freshman, having skipped eighth grade like many graduates of St. Joseph's. This made me younger than most of the girls in my class, but because of my height and physical development, the difference was not readily apparent. I was one of five new African American girls, a veritable wave of diversity in a school that just the year before had counted only four African Americans among its student body of about 250.

Dobbs was a boarding school, but my mother did not want and could not afford for me to board. So every morning I had to rise before the sun to catch the bus at 5:45 A.M. My poor mother would come to my room, flip on the light, and plead with me, "Ilyasah, would you please wake up? You're going to miss the bus."

"It's too early!" I'd cry, pulling a pillow over my head.

The bus drove all over lower Westchester picking up day girls, as we were called to distinguish us from the boarding students. There were about fifteen of us, scattered throughout Bronxville, Scarsdale, Hartsdale, White Plains. I was the only one from Mount Vernon.

There were things I liked about Dobbs. I liked occasionally spending the night with my friend Karole Dill in one of the dorms. Karole was, like me, younger than our classmates and very, very smart. My mother loved her because on the day we first came to visit Dobbs, Karole took us on a tour of the school. My mother was already impressed by this bright, young sister who seemed so confident and self-assured. And then we got to Karole's room and there, hanging proudly on the wall, was a big poster of my father. It turned out Karole had studied *Malcolm X Speaks* as a young child in summer school at Uhuru Sasa School at The East in Brooklyn. Once my mother heard this bit of information, Karole was in.

I enjoyed assembly, when the entire school community would gather in the auditorium each morning to hear guest speakers or have a school discussion on some topic. I liked my English teacher, Miss Marks, though she was pale and nervous and always slightly startled, like a bird. Nonetheless she introduced us to Thoreau and

Salinger and in class we would veer off into wide-ranging discussions about life and the meaning thereof. I loved my dance instructor, Marlene Furtek, and the classes in modern, tap, and ballet. I loved my French instructor, Madame Davidson, and French class where the desks had earphones that let you hear the lesson translated at just your speed.

What I did not like about Dobbs was American history class; it was boring and mundane and in those stories of brave white men fighting for their freedom I saw no relevance to my life. I didn't care about the Revolutionary War or Thomas Jefferson or George Washington. To me, American history was boring and dark and depressing.

What I also disliked about Dobbs was having to come home each afternoon on the bus, riding through the neighborhood like some big dork, the only black face among a sea of white people. It wasn't being among whites that embarrassed me, it was the high visibility, the disconnected nature of coming home at a different time in a different way from a different school. When the bus turned the corner onto the tree-lined streets of my neighborhood, I would slouch down low in my seat, praying my friends would stay inside their homes for the minutes it would take me to race from the bus to my front door.

But it was while I was a student at Dobbs that I began to emerge from the protective cocoon Mommy had spun for all of us. Sometimes I joke that my mother raised six princesses, or six kept women—that's how much she satisfied our every need and desire, and kept us sheltered from the outside. She kept us so sheltered that we grew up with little understanding of how difficult, and even cruel, the world could be. But by my fourteenth year, I began to understand.

When I was twelve or so, a girl named Deirdre moved into her grandmother's house on East 5th Street, two blocks from our house, and because she was my age and because she was so nice, we quickly became friends. Deirdre was tall and caramel-colored and beautiful; she looked like a young Vanessa Williams, only much prettier. She was so pretty that a lot of girls hated her.

One day as we were walking up East 5th Street toward my house, a group of girls appeared out of nowhere and began calling our names. Although we knew them and they knew us, these were not girls from our neighborhood. They were from the South Side and they were tough girls, gang girls, all fists and nails and attitude. They called themselves the Chain Gang and had taken to hanging around our community because one of them, Sharon, had a crush on my friend Tony Abney. Tony was very popular.

They walked toward us, calling our names and smiling all the while. "Hey, Yasah, we just want to talk to Deirdre a minute, just a minute, don't worry, come on." Before I realized what was happening, they had Deirdre on the ground, smashing her with their fists and ripping off her clothes. By the time I jumped into the crowd, Deirdre was a screaming, crying mess. Her shirt was gone, her bra exposed. The fox coat she'd been wearing looked like the pelt of a mangy dog. I got the girls off her but only because they were finished anyway. They walked off, laughing. One of the girls, her name was Carol, called back a parting shot. "Guess you don't think you're all that cute now."

I don't know who was more shocked, Deirdre or me. I couldn't get over the fact that they'd beat her up just because she was beautiful.

One day I decided to give Tony Abney a present. We were good friends; Tony treated me like a little sister and I looked up to him and wanted to thank him for being so nice to me. At any rate, when I decided to give him a present, I walked into the campus bookstore at Dobbs and found this beautiful hunter green leather-bound journal. I charged it, the way I charged a hundred things at the store, not understanding my mother had to pay those charges at the end of each month.

And so, I inscribed the book "To Tony, love, Yasah," and gave it to him. A few days later a girl appeared at our front door, asking for me. It was Sharon from the South Side. She looked me up and down, curled her lip, then held out Tony's journal as if it were a snake. "What the hell do you think you're doing giving my man this book?" she asked.

Although she was clearly threatening me, I wasn't frightened, only confused. *Her* man? What did that mean? Why couldn't I give my friend a present if I wanted to? What difference did it make to her? I didn't know anything about jealousy. I didn't know anything about possessiveness. I had never experienced the deep, violent fear of a teenage girl who thought she might lose the one thing of value in her life. So I said, "Tony's my friend. If I want to give him a book, I will."

The next thing I knew, the Chain Gang was looking to jump me. I managed to avoid them for a while, but one day as Gamilah and I were walking home from the train station we saw, up ahead of us, a girl named Charmaine. I was instantly on alert, because I knew she was Sharon's best friend. But Charmaine just smiled and waved and went on her way. After a few minutes, I relaxed. Maybe the Chain Gang had taken me off their list.

We rounded the corner to our street, walked two blocks, and stopped in our tracks. There, at the side entrance to my house, stood a group of girls waiting for us. Apparently Charmaine had smiled to lure us into a false sense of security, then run onto the block and sounded the alarm: "Yo, Sharon! Yasah and Gamilah are on their way down the street!" By the time we approached the Cedar Avenue corner of our house, there they stood.

"What are we going to do?" Gamilah asked. She was terrified. She couldn't let that gang beat up her sister, but she didn't want to fight either.

"I don't know." If we ran, they would catch us and beat us. If we kept walking, they'd catch us and beat us. There didn't seem to be a good solution either way.

But just as we were about to raise our fists and give up hope, Mommy appeared like an angel, walking down the last set of stairs from our front door. At the sight of her, my eyes flooded with tears of relief. Speaking with firmness but warmth, she told the girls to go home, there would be no fighting that day or any day, we could not afford to fight ourselves when there was so much injustice against African people all over the world that needed to be fought. She was wearing a nightgown and robe, but I thought she looked more majestic than I had ever seen her look and my heart flooded with love. The tension in the air dissolved instantly. One by one, the girls wandered off down the street. They weren't happy, but no one threatened us or spoke to us or said anything disrespectful.

They just turned and left. Gamilah and I went inside, and later, when Qubilah came home, I told her how frightened I had been. She told me if anyone ever tried to beat me up, the best line of defense was to act crazy, to start swinging wildly and grunting and screaming and, if possible, foaming at the mouth. Then they would leave me alone.

I never did get jumped by the Chain Gang, thank God. I stayed close to home for a few days, then avoided Sharon and Charmaine and the others altogether for a few weeks, and after awhile my name got pushed down on the Chain Gang Hate List, replaced by some other soul who made the mistake of smiling at somebody's boyfriend, or thinking herself cute, or being smart and showing it, or otherwise trying to live her turbulent adolescent life.

Later on, after I'd graduated from college and was living on my own, I ran into one of the old Chain Gang members. Her hair was brittle and broken, her face was worn, and in one of her fights, she had chipped a front tooth. She looked exhausted, though it was only eight o'clock in the morning, and I was going to pretend not to see her as we passed in the restaurant parking lot, not for my sake but for hers. But she recognized me and smiled and I smiled back and waved. We both said hello.

Michael Peeples was the hustle king of Lower Westchester County and, at thirteen, I was his queen. Michael was like Fred Astaire with soul, John Travolta with funk. Everybody wanted to dance with Michael, everybody wanted to be his partner, but he chose me.

He was two years older than me, a tall, good-looking, ebony young man of Caribbean descent. He was wildly popular and dated lots of girls, including my friend Lisa and my play cousin Simone, but he always treated me like a little sister and I looked up to him as a trusted friend. My mother liked him so much she allowed him to escort me to parties when no one else could.

We would practice in each other's living rooms on Saturdays, perfecting our steps, working our groove. Then, on Saturday night, we hit the town: dances at Mount Vernon high, clubs like the T-Connection in the Bronx and the Diamond J in White Plains. Everywhere we went, we stole the show. Michael always wore a three-piece suit; I wore shimmery little disco dresses and tried not to trip in my platform shoes. (It actually happened once, at the T-Connection. We had just finished dancing and were leaving and I skidded in my brand-new, very grown-up high heels and slid on my bottom all the way down a flight of stairs.)

It was all very *Saturday Night Fever*. We'd step into the ballroom with the music blasting and the mirrored ball spinning and the colored lights flashing, and it was all so exciting for a young girl. The dance floor would be packed with couples shaking their stuff, but when Michael grabbed my hand and spun me around, the crowds parted. We danced our little hearts out.

Sometimes, driving to or from one of the dances, we would stop at a traffic light, jump out of the car, hustle a bit in the glow of our headlights, then jump back in and drive away. Other times Michael would steer the car to some brightly lit parking lot, say the one of the local Corvette dealership, and we'd jump out, dance a few steps for the surprised salesmen, then get back in the car and roar off into the night, laughing all the way.

I took my hustle queen title with me to Dobbs and taught my

friends there how to dance. On Saturday nights, when the school held dances with boys from Lawrenceville or Trinity-Pawling, the African American students held alternative dances downstairs in a common room. My friend Tony Abney would bring his records and some friends from the neighborhood. While the rest of the school was rocking to Bruce Springsteen, we were getting down to Stevie Wonder and the Bee Gees. Even after I left Dobbs, the boys from Mount Vernon continued to serve as stand-in boyfriends for the African American girls there, providing music at their parties and escorting the girls to their proms. Karole told me the introduction to my neighborhood completely changed her Dobbs social life.

At the same time I was dancing my way across Westchester County I was also hoping to become the next Beverly Johnson. When I was thirteen years old a woman who ran a local modeling agency approached my mother and asked if I had ever considered modeling. Naturally, I was thrilled; I immediately saw myself strolling down the runways of Paris and posing for the cover of *Vogue*.

Unfortunately, Mommy was less enthusiastic about the idea. "She needs to finish high school first," she told the woman, gently but firmly shooing her away. To soothe my disappointment Mommy enrolled me in a Barbizon School of Modeling, but it was mainly a distraction. She wanted me to focus on my education and not be swept away by dreams of making it big in the fashion world.

Still, I enjoyed the classes in makeup, fashion design, poise, and carriage. Throughout high school I did some small runway work, modeling in the occasional mall or charity fashion show, including one at the United Nations. When I finished high school the same woman suggested I try modeling again. "She needs to go to college first," Mommy said. When I finished college, the woman asked a third time. "She needs to get her master's degree," Mommy said.

At that point, taking matters into my own hands, I made an appointment with someone at the Ford Agency. She was a polite but crisp woman who looked me up and down and took less than five minutes to tell me to forget it. It was like, "Next!"

So ended my modeling career.

Roots

*or African Americans of my generation, **Roots** was like the
assassination of John F. Kennedy: Everybody can remember
where they were and what they were doing when the momen-
tous event took place.*

I was fourteen years old and a student at Dobbs. It was a cold
week at the end of January and I happened to be staying in the
dorm with my friend Karole Dill, which meant that she and I
watched the miniseries in a room full of white girls. Every night
at nine o'clock we all thundered down to the common room,
switched on the television, and, like millions of Americans, were
swept away by the horror that was slavery and the bravery and forti-
tude of those who were slaves. I don't know how the white girls in
the room felt—probably they were as shocked as Karole, Veronica,
Angela, Kathy, Sandy, and I. Maybe they were also a little ashamed.
But I know exactly how we felt: We were horrified. Certainly we
knew there had been slavery. I knew, from my lessons with Brother

Tawfiq and from Mommy, that slavery had stripped our true heritage from us. But knowing about slavery in a disconnected, intellectual way and seeing it portrayed so vividly are two very different things, especially to fourteen-year-old girls. Seeing the loving and dignified African family that welcomed the baby Kunta into the world filled us with pride (even though the "bush" setting may not have been accurate), but watching our people so abused and degraded night after night filled us with pain. Every night it got worse and worse. Kunta Kinte, handsome and happy and free, being hunted and trapped like an animal and stolen from his home. Kunta Kinte, brutally whipped and hanging from a beam, finally forced to submit, at least outwardly, to the name "Toby." Kizzy being sold off the plantation and dragged from her parents' arms.

Every night, when the episode ended, I would stagger up from the television in a kind of daze, raw and alienated from girls who, only hours before, had been my friends. And the next day, as I walked around the dorm and the campus staring at the paintings of great white men and women on the walls, I would wonder: Did you do this, too?

What's interesting is that I recall absolutely no discussion about the miniseries, not one word. You might think such a vivid re-creation of history would be a perfect launching pad for a frank conversation about slavery and race relations in America and that one of the teachers, if not one of us girls, would initiate it. But no, no one said a thing.

Perhaps partly in response, all of us girls of color tried to reach out to our brothers and sisters. We volunteered to tutor the younger African Americans and Latinas who were placed at various foster care and juvenile facilities in Dobbs Ferry. Working with these girls I found that I identified with them more than I thought I would. In a real way, their existence was mine.

The following summer I went to camp in Vermont and realized for the first time on a conscious level how few African Americans were around. The realization did not upset me; I still loved camp and had a great time. But once a person steps into the bright light of awareness it's hard to go back into the shadows. And so that was my last year at Camp Betsey Cox.

By my tenth-grade year at Dobbs, Attallah and Qubilah had both begun college, while Gamilah, Malikah, and Malaak were all in private schools. Although my mother was employed as an associate professor of health administration at Medgar Evers College, she was still having trouble keeping up with all the tuition payments. At one point she called on her adopted mother, Helen Malloy, to help pay my bill at Dobbs.

After two years, I left Dobbs and enrolled at the Scarborough Country Day school. Mommy never specified the reason for the change, but I assumed it was my oft-stated wish to go to school with boys. I had enjoyed my two years at Dobbs, but its single-sex status felt limiting and unrealistic. Not that I was boy-crazy; I was still a little scared of the whole mating dance. But I wanted to be in a school that felt a little more like the real world.

The Scarborough Country Day school was about fifteen miles from Dobbs. Scarborough was smaller than Dobbs, with fewer students and a campus that was more quaint than grand. These classrooms were older than those at Dobbs, with wooden desks and less high technology. The teachers had long hair and said "Groovy."

The students were as wealthy as those at Dobbs, but seemed to come from families where the parents seemed largely too busy or too distracted to notice the many ways in which their teenage children were amusing themselves. Everyone had long hair and loved Led Zeppelin and the Grateful Dead and hated disco; a sign above the stereo in the foggy smoking room read "Disco Sucks!" And tobacco was not the only thing being smoked at Scarborough Country Day.

There were only a handful of black students at Scarborough, but no one made a big deal of it. I made friends with a girl named Joy, and in our discussions of the issue, we decided Scarborough was fine but we both wanted to attend historically black colleges. It was while I was at Scarborough that the father of a friend of mine, Jon Usadi, pulled me into his study and, like my friend Lisa Anthony's father had, told me how great a man my father was, how admirable he was, and how significant his contributions were to humanity. I thought that was very nice.

I also made friends with a white girl named Debi who lived in Scarsdale and rode the schoolbus with me. Debi was very pretty and very cool. Her mother kept her nails and her hair "done." We were only fifteen, but she came to school with hair like Farrah Fawcett's and nails that never saw a chip or a nick and changed colors every week. I was so impressed that one Friday I went home and did my nails. The following Monday I strolled into the lounge and Debi took one look and loudly said, "Oh, Yasah. What did you do—get Lee Press-ons?" I said "Yeah" as nonchalantly as I could and chuckled, but my feelings were hurt. I wasn't that crazy about her afterward.

Michelle Weiss was the most popular girl at Scarborough. She was blonde and pert and pretty, and one day she invited a group of us to her house for lunch. We ate sitting around the pool in the backyard of her Chappaqua home, and some of the kids drank so much I thought they would never be able to go back to school after lunch. But they did.

Some days Attallah would pick me up and take me out to lunch. She was attending Manhattanville College and lived nearby, so it was an easy drive for her. I'd sit on the bench outside the main building, a structure that looked like a smaller version of the White House, and watch Attallah drive up in her little Volkswagen bug. I was so proud of my beautiful big sister, and impressed with the way she whipped that little bug around the narrow country roads of upper Westchester County.

The basketball coach at Scarborough somehow got it into his mind that because I was tall (five feet ten inches) I should join the basketball team. Most of the girls on the team were in excited agreement, Michelle and Cheryll among them. I protested that I, in fact, did not know how to play basketball, had never dribbled a ball, and had never taken a shot in my life. They didn't believe me.

"All you have to do is run up and down the court," they said. They seemed to believe that once I laced up my shoes, the spirit of the Harlem Globetrotters would take over and I would be knocking down shots with the best of them. And they were so insistent I finally gave in.

In the locker room before my first game I watched a few of my teammates warm up by doing shots of Southern Comfort. Then we ran out onto the floor and shook hands with our visitors, a team from a local Catholic school. The ref blew the whistle and the game began. Heart pounding already, I started running up and down the court, just like I'd been told to do. Everybody else was playing ball, but I was running up and down the court, up and down, praying no one was stupid enough to pass the basketball to me. Behind me, I heard Michelle's voice, low and vicious.

"Get out of my way, you fucking spic!" she hissed.

For a moment I was confused. What was she talking about? Then I looked at the players from the other team—I'd been too nervous to really look at them before—and realized several of the girls were Latina.

"Fucking greaseball," Michelle hissed again in a clutch.

I was too stunned to say anything, so I just began to run slowly up and down, up and down the court, completely bewildered. Sometimes one of my teammates would try to pass the ball to me. But I either lost it or dropped it or just passed it as quickly as I could and, after awhile, they gave up. When I announced the next day that I was quitting the team, nobody tried to stop me.

My mother visited the school one day and saw a couple of students wandering around, long-haired and glassy-eyed. She took me out of there after one year.

In 1978, at the age of fifteen, I entered my third and final high school: the Hackley Preparatory School in Tarrytown. Hackley was a lot more like Dobbs than Scarborough Country Day. It had a big, beautiful campus and a larger student body; it was old and historic and had once been an all-boys school. There was a dress code: Boys had to wear a coat and tie and could not wear blue jeans. The girls' dress code was harder to define. Basically we were forbidden to wear tight, revealing dresses or any manner of seductive dress. But I remember occasionally slipping past in one of my disco dresses—

one pink and one ice blue—and struggling up the long, steep hill to the academic building in high heels. It was ridiculous.

Again, I was among only a handful of black students at Hackley. Gordon Parks's daughter Leslie was there in the lower school, and there were two other girls in my senior class, one of whom was in the same chapter of Jack and Jill as I was. There was a boy named Ashley one year behind me; he played on the football team and was very popular.

And there was a senior named Benji. They called him Fuck-'Em-and-Chuck-'Em Benji, for reasons that are self-explanatory. Benji dated only white girls, which may have bothered some African American girls on other campuses but which secretly made me glad. I didn't want him practicing his love-'em-and-leave-'em techniques on me.

Interracial dating is a touchy subject, one of those topics that can raise hackles on all sides. The sight of a black man and a white woman or a white man and a black woman strolling hand in hand pushes more buttons in many Americans than an accordionist— fear, guilt, anger, self-loathing, echos of subjugation and exploitation, centuries and centuries of pain. People who don't know me sometimes assume I hold strong views on the topic; they expect the daughter of Malcolm X to be right out front of the segregationist parade, waving the flag for sticking with one's own kind. It is true that my father once preached against integration in general, and interracial marriage in particular, believing there were so many other issues we needed to resolve. That was a stage in his progression and learning, in his assimilation of the varied influences upon his life. One of the truly remarkable things about my father was his capacity for change, for self-improvement and self-analysis. His whole life, especially the latter part of it, was a journey. He was a man who embraced new worlds, new scenery, new ideas. Remember, he was only thirty-nine when he was assassinated, and in those thirty-nine years he never stagnated, but grew and grew.

Make no mistake: I'm not making excuses for my father, nor apologizing for him. Malcolm X needs no one to make excuses for him. There was the constant refrain that Daddy was changing his beliefs toward the end of his life, an idea at which Mommy scoffed. She said my father used to say that people, especially white people, had pompous gall to insist that he change before white people changed their treatment of African Americans. But in traveling to Mecca and experiencing, for the first time in his American life, true brotherhood with people of all skin colors and hues, my father was blessed with a deeper understanding of humanity. And he was a big enough man to accept that understanding, even if it conflicted with his previous views.

In his last television interview with Canadian journalist Pierre Berton in Toronto, one month before he was killed, my father said, "I believe in recognizing every human being as a human being, neither white, black, brown, nor red. When you are dealing with humanity as one family, there's no question of integration or intermarriage. It's just one human being marrying another human being, or one human being living around and with another human being. I must say, though, that I don't think the burden to defend any such position should ever be put upon the black man. Because it is the white man collectively who has shown that he is hostile towards integration and towards intermarriage and towards these other strides towards oneness. So, as a black man, and especially as a black American, I don't think that I would have to defend any stand that I formerly took. Because it's still a reaction of the society and it's a reaction that was produced by the white society."

My feeling about interracial dating is this: It's a matter of personal choice. I have never dated a white man, though I have been attracted to a few. I thought Peter Brady on "The Brady Bunch" was cute, Keith Partridge was sexy, and Davy from the Monkees had a nice way of swinging that hair. At Scarborough there was a boy named Bill who had brown hair, a sweet smile, and made my heart speed up whenever he said hello. But he never asked me out and I never did anything to make him think I would be receptive to the idea. At Hackley I admired the looks of Rick Romero and Bill Wolman. But something always held me back from white men; something always told me no. Some of my friends have dated white men and still do; I say God bless them. If you can find someone to love in this world, why would you hesitate to embrace that person based simply on the color of his skin?

I am bothered, however, by those who are in interracial relationships simply to be with a person of another ethnic group. If an attraction is based on the complexion of the skin rather than the content of the character, if a person wants just to have a white woman because she's white or a black man because he's black, that bothers me.

Here's a story about my father, told by Dr. Dorothy Height, chair and president emerita of the National Council of Negro Women:

"I can never forget the time when the United Civil Rights

Leadership was called to come to Pleasantville, New York, by Ossie Davis, Ruby Dee, and Sidney Poitier shortly after Malcolm X returned from Mecca. Malcolm wanted to talk, and he asked them to bring us all together. He explained that too much effort was put on dealing with white prejudice, and he thought that much more attention needed to be put on black unity and on our learning to work together.

"I remember that Lorraine Hansberry was lying on a couch when Malcolm said that we needed to talk to each other and not about each other through the press. She leaned up and said, 'Well, Malcolm, I agree with you, but how do you think I felt lying in a hospital fighting for my life and I heard you say I was disloyal to my race because I married a white man? You didn't ask me who he was or what I knew about him or why I married him.' And Malcolm just said, very gently, 'You're perfectly right, sister.'

"And that was all he said."

It was at Hackley that I first heard a white person use the word *nigger* in my presence. I was hanging out in the recreation room with my friends Liz, Paola, Kristene, Andi, and Michelle. They were sweet girls; we got along famously, consumed, as we all were, with boys and fashion and grades and scoring as high as possible on the SAT. I don't think the subject of race had ever been raised between us.

Until that afternoon, Liz, flicking back her hair and rolling her eyes for dramatic purposes, mentioned that someone had broken into her father's car. It happened while she and some friends were down in the Village the previous weekend, and since she'd been driving, her father blamed her. He was making her pay for the smashed window out of her own pocket. Liz was incensed.

We all clucked in sympathy. "That's too bad. Did they take anything? At least they didn't steal the car."

"That's true," Liz said. "But it makes me so mad. How dare those niggers break into my father's car like that?"

At first I thought I must have misheard her. But then I felt the room go silent and still and when I glanced up, I saw everyone except Liz was looking at me. She was still caught up in her fit of pique.

"Those niggers should be arrested. I wish there were something I could do."

Nobody said anything, nobody breathed. After a few moments, Liz must have realized something was wrong. She followed everyone's glance and found me, finally seeming to remember I was in the room.

"Oh, Yasah, you know I don't mean you," she said with a smile.

I was nearly too stunned to speak, but I managed to say, "I don't like that word, Liz."

"But those guys were niggers," Liz insisted. "You know they were. But you're not. After all, you're not *black-black*."

I didn't know whether to laugh, yell, or stand up and walk out. I was not hurt, not in the way so many of us can be hurt by the use of that word, because I knew the true history of Africans and I knew that word was an attempt to obliterate that proud history. What I couldn't figure out was why Liz was using it so casually? She was a nice girl; I had never seen even the trace of prejudice in her. She was, I thought, my friend.

Confused and surprised, I tried to explain to Liz why what she was saying was wrong. But she dug in her heels, insisting the word was okay when used for the kind of people who would break into cars. Over and over she repeated that it didn't refer to me because I wasn't "black-black." Whatever that meant. How she even knew the person who had smashed her father's window was of color was never established. After awhile someone steered the conversation in another direction, much to the relief of all concerned, and everybody pretended the incident never happened.

But things weren't the same between me and Liz after that. We still smiled and said hello when we met in the hallway and even still hung out with the same group of friends sometimes. But I looked at her differently now. I wasn't angry and I did not dislike her, but whatever true, human connection had once been between us was gone. And she knew it.

Sometimes I'd catch Liz looking at me when she thought I wasn't looking. Maybe she was ashamed of her behavior or guilty. Maybe she was thinking I had turned out to be, in fact, "black-black." I don't know what she was thinking because I never asked. She looked at me and I looked at her and then, eventually, one of us turned away.

Boys

W**hen I was a young girl I didn't think of myself as
pretty.** I didn't think of myself as ugly either—no
one had ever made me feel unattractive in the slight-
est way. It was more that I just didn't think of myself as a *girl*, per
se. I was Ilyasah, daughter of two, sister of five, friend to many. The
whole concept of attractiveness and its importance in one's life
took some time to be borne upon me.

There were plenty of girly things that I enjoyed. I liked pretty
clothes and sharp outfits, just like the rest of my sisters. I doodled
with the best of them, decorating my notebooks with flowers and
stars and fanciful drawings of my name or the names I wished I
had: Cookie, Pumpkin, Angela. I liked having my hair combed and
styled, and when Attallah cut my first bangs I was thrilled; I drew a
picture of myself as the famous Marlo Thomas, with the signature
bangs and that feisty little flip of the hair. I certainly knew that
beauty existed—Mommy was beautiful and Attallah was stunning,
her golden-brown Afro waving proudly as she strode down the

street with her distinctive strut. But it never occurred to me to apply the measuring stick of beauty to my own face.

Once, when I was about fourteen, my sister Attallah drew a picture of a girl with long, black hair and almond-shaped eyes and nice lips. "Wow, who is that?" I asked. "She's so pretty."

"That's you, silly," Attallah said.

I think at least part of the reason for my state of suspended animation lay with my reluctance to jump feet first into the whole confusing world of boys. As I entered adolescence the male body was like some vast, unknown country to me, not only unexplored but largely unseen. There were plenty of male role models circling the orbit of my life—my grandfather and uncles and the fathers of close friends—but my home world was all female.

I knew about breasts because Mommy had them and so did Aunt Ruth and Attallah sprouted hers when I was about eight. Later, I begged Qubilah to show me hers but instead she drew a picture, pretending they had hair and pimples on them. She made it sound so terrible I declared I didn't want "those things" growing on me. I slept in a bra, thinking that would help.

But I knew nothing about the anatomy of boys. Ellis Hazlip, a family friend and host of the television show "Soul" in the late 1960s and 1970s, sometimes visited our house with the singer-songwriter Curtis Mayfield. Mr. Hazlip liked to wear tight pants that left little to the imagination. Qubilah and I would stare at the strange bulge below his belly in astonishment. *What the hell was that thing, anyway? Had he swallowed something enormous? Did he have some kind of growth?* We would giggle so hard we had to leave the room.

Mommy never talked to me about the birds and the bees,

never explained the sexual workings of the human body, probably because she was too busy attending to more pressing needs. Had I asked, I know she would have patiently sat me down, but I never asked because I never thought to. Why should I? What was there to know? I'd had a "boyfriend" since I was six, a relationship that largely consisted of speaking to one another at the mosque. No big deal.

But as I entered high school, I sensed a change in this state of nonchalance between the sexes, and I knew I was not ready for whatever was to come. I was nearly two years younger than most of the girls in my class at Dobbs, and much more naive than many of my friends or the girls from the south side of Mount Vernon who came to hang out in our neighborhood. Boys began teasing me about my stiff, unsexy walk. I was perplexed; I walked the way I had always walked.

"Girls are supposed to roll their hips," they said. "Be like Attallah." Attallah was tall and stately and self-assured and had a walk so sexy it made boys want to sit down and cry.

For her part, Attallah tried to help by handing out advice on crucial activities like the fine art of French kissing. She demonstrated the proper technique by making an "O" with the tips of her thumb and index finger, then sticking a piece of chewing gum to her pinky. You were supposed to put your mouth to the circle of your fingers, then reach for the gum with your tongue. The idea made my head swim.

Parties, in particular, worried me. All those teenage hormones flying around somebody's hot, sweaty basement; I didn't know what to do with myself. I went to one with Qubilah, whose friends all attended the United Nations school and were into David Bowie and The Police and were mostly white. While she danced and socialized the night away, I spent the evening in a chair, just gazing around.

At another party, this one thrown by my friend Robin Johnson, the lights were turned down so low all the bodies on the dance floor looked like one, big gyrating blob. Whenever a boy asked me to dance, I shook my head. "No, thanks." There was no way I was getting out there in the darkness. After awhile the boys stopped asking, which was fine with me. I spent the evening sitting on the steps with two much younger girls, weaving potholders with brightly colored skeins of yarn.

When I was fourteen a boy named Edgar gave me my first real kiss. Edgar looked like Tupac. He was cool and sexy, with shiny black hair. He lived with his mother in Harlem but visited his father, stepmother, and older brother Leon in Mount Vernon on weekends. Edgar would come to my friend Tony's house, where Michael Peeples and I would be practicing our hustle routine. After awhile people began calling Edgar my boyfriend. I didn't mind. Edgar was handsome and sweet to me and he gave me a gold ring with a huge, pale blue stone in the middle. I was thrilled, until the band began to change colors. Then I panicked, thinking I had somehow ruined a perfectly good gold ring. I put it away in my dresser, hoping Edgar wouldn't notice. He never did.

Edgar and I were good friends as much as anything, there for each other during the tough times as well as the good. I used to talk to his mother on the telephone; she was very sweet. And when Edgar's brother Leon went off to serve a stint in the armed forces, we all got together to say good-bye and to comfort Edgar. We knew how he felt because Leon was like a brother to us all; the idea of him leaving and breaking up the group was hard. I think we all sensed that the little family we'd created would never be the same, that eventually, one by one, we would all head off on different paths. After we said our good-byes, I went home and spent the entire evening in my bedroom, looking out my window at the summer trees, crying like a baby at the thought of losing him.

But we kept on hanging and kept on hustling. One day, after my friends Jackie Grant, Simone Davis, Lisa Anthony, and I had hustled all afternoon at Tony's house, Edgar offered to walk me home. As we were leaving, Edgar announced that he was going to kiss me. He said it so matter-of-factly he might have been discussing the weather and I responded in the same vein.

"Okay," I said.

We walked outside and Edgar turned to me. He wasn't a short boy but I was tall for my age and so had at least four inches on him. "Wait a minute," he said, leading me back to the stairs. He walked up two steps, pulled me toward him and leaned in.

"Close your eyes," he said.

I did and felt something warm and soft pressed against my lips. Despite Attallah's instructions I had no intention of opening my mouth. We pressed lips for a few minutes, then Edgar walked me home and I pretty much forgot about it. Edgar and I went out for a few more months, then we drifted apart.

And yet, as naive and wary of boys as I was, I knew very well the words of adult encounters. I knew the word *sex* and several of its slang counterparts. I knew the names of the pertinent body parts. More important, I knew the word *love* and what it was supposed to mean. And I knew the word *rape*.

I remember being as young as twelve and warning my girlfriends at St. Joseph Montessori School that if anyone ever tried to rape them, they should go along with it. Better to be raped than be killed, I said sagely. Where I got this information, I don't know. Maybe I saw it on TV. Maybe one of my female relatives whispered it into my ear, though that I doubt. Whatever the source of this knowledge, it had lodged in a back part of my brain.

There was another girl in my class at St. Joseph's. Her name was Carla and she lived in the northern Bronx, in a towering housing complex. We were friends; her mother took me, Lisa, Monique, and Kim to Madison Square Garden to see the Jackson Five in concert. We kept in touch even after leaving St. Joseph's, and so it was that she invited me to a party when I was fourteen.

My mother drove me, Gamilah, and my friend Lisa to Carla's house and dropped us off. It was early in the evening; the party had yet to begin, but the boy who was going to be the DJ was there. He said he had to go home to get his records and he asked me to come along. It didn't occur to me to say no.

He told me his records were at his sister's house and we started to walk. It seemed to take forever to reach the house, and when we got there, no one was home.

"Don't you have a key?" I asked.

"Nah," he said. "Let's go to my friend's house. He has some of my records there."

We walked some more, to another house. No answer there

either. By now I was starting to get a little tired and I wanted to get back to the party, but I had no idea where I was. I didn't know the Bronx and I couldn't just wander off by myself.

"One more stop," he said. This time it was an apartment building. We started climbing stairs and then, all of a sudden, the stairs stopped. There was only a heavy metal door before us. He pushed it open and the next thing I knew we were standing on the roof.

"Pull down your pants," he ordered, no longer the smiling boy I'd first met.

My heart seized. I wanted to scream but fear caught the sound in my throat. My mind reeled back and forth like a drunk, confused, unsure. I didn't know what was going on but something told me to do what he wanted, just go along and get out alive. I had seen no one else as we climbed the stairs; for all I knew we were alone in the building. Alone in the world.

He put his hand over my mouth and pushed me up against the door. I lay beneath him, stiff and dazed. When it was all over, he pushed himself off me and zipped his pants. I pulled myself up straight and stood there, too stunned to think or move or pull up my pants. "Come on," he said roughly, trying to pull me back down the stairs. I stumbled.

"Pull up your pants," he ordered. I did. We started down the stairs, but it was hard for me to walk. The inside of my thighs burned in a way I had never felt before and something wet trickled into my panties.

"I'm bleeding," I told him.

"Shut up," he said. "That's sperm."

Somehow we stumbled out of the building and made our way back to the party. We didn't speak as we walked and my mind would not consider what had just happened. I just kept wondering if he was going to get the records, but he never did.

Back at the party Lisa asked me why I was walking funny. I made up some story and got through the night. What happened after that, I don't remember, except I do remember going home and calling my friend Tony to tell him I wasn't a virgin anymore. I told him I hurt. He told me to sit in a tub of warm water to ease the pain and so I did. I didn't cry or try to purge myself the way some rape victims do because I didn't know that what happened to me was, in fact, rape. I didn't blame myself or the boy, just sat in the tub trying to still both body and mind. Was that sex? Was that what it was supposed to be like between a girl and a boy? I was very confused.

I never told Carla or my sisters. I never even considered telling Mommy because I didn't know how she might react. All I wanted was to forget that moment on the roof had ever occurred. I didn't want to focus on it; I wanted that night eliminated from the corners of my mind and, for the most part, I succeeded. But, every now and then at Dobbs, when the girls were all sitting around talking about sex, I would think of that night on the rooftop. What had happened to me had not felt like "making love." It hadn't even felt like having sex, but sometimes I pretended it had been because pretending made it easier to take. So I pretended and tried to fit in and impress the other girls with my maturity by laughing and chiming in to the conversation. Talking about my man and his "thing."

———

Around about this same time I fell in love for the first time in my life. His name was Howie. He was a pretty boy, a singer and performer who did not mind that he was nine years older than me. In fact, Howie decided it was his job to teach me the ways of a sophisticated adult. He was the first man who made love to me, I think. He told me I shouldn't wear white tube socks with black shoes. He showed me off to his friends. He used to sing "Chocolate Girl" by the Whispers to me. He gave me my first drink. We were at his house, sitting in the living room listening to Isaac Hayes and Barry White and holding hands. He got up to make himself a drink and came back to the couch holding two screwdrivers.

"You know, you really should begin to acquire a taste for this," he said.

"I'm ready," I said and took the glass. I had never tasted alcohol. I had tried pot once, but I didn't like how sleepy and paranoid it made me feel and decided it was for losers. But if Howie thought I should acquire a taste for cocktails, I was willing to try.

I drank the whole glass, fooled by the taste of the orange juice, and promptly got sick as a dog. Howie drove me home, probably scared as all hell, and put me into bed. Luckily my mother wasn't home—that time. But later, when she found out about Howie, she hit the ceiling. She forbade me to see him, which, of course, just made me want to see him more. I was in love; I thought Howie was *the* man for the rest of my life. I naively assumed we would get married someday. That was how these things happened, wasn't it? You went to college and made a career so you could be a good partner, a contributor who had something to offer a man. Then you met the man, you fell in love, you married him and stayed

together for the rest of your lives while you both contributed to society. That was how my parents had done it, and that was my tem-
plate. Being still in high school, I was a little ahead of the curve
with Howie, but I thought the game would be played out the
same way.

Howie could not come to my house when Mommy was home.
But Mommy went away on a long trip to Africa and Aunt Ruth
was less concerned about these things. Howie came over and we sat
in the living room on the couch, kissing and talking and holding
hands. After awhile, we fell asleep. I woke to Qubilah's urgent
shaking.

"Wake up!" she said. "Mommy's home!"

It was too late. Mommy walked into the living room just as I was
wiping the sleep from my eyes. Later she told me she took one look
at that twenty-four-year-old man wrapped around her fifteen-year-
old daughter and saw red.

"Get out of my house!" she yelled. "She's a child! You're a
grown man! You should be ashamed of yourself!" Mommy chased
Howie out of the house and down the stairs to the street.

But I kept seeing Howie, despite what Mommy thought. I was
in love and I didn't care. We dated for nearly two years, seeing each
other even after I had gone away to college. We dated until one day
a friend told me Howie was seeing another girl on the side.

I was devastated, completely devastated. I cried for days and
wandered through my school hours in a daze. Walking home
through the woods, I looked to God, wondering how such a thing
could happen, feeling as though someone had punched into my
chest and grabbed my heart with his fist. I felt as if my whole life
had ended at the age of seventeen and there was nothing I could do

about it. I knew in my heart I could not be with Howie anymore, though it was painful, because he had cheated on me.

He came to my house to try to persuade me not to end the relationship.

"You're like my right arm," Howie said. "If I lose you I feel like I'm losing a part of myself."

I thought that was the most profound thing anyone would ever say to me, and it made me cry so hard I couldn't breathe. Howie pulled me into his arms and it felt so safe there, so warm and secure, I wanted to remain forever. But I pulled myself away.

"Howie . . ." I began.

He cut me off. "Baby, come on. Please don't do this."

It was killing me, hearing the pain in his voice. "Please go," I said.

"Baby . . ."

"Howie, you need to leave!"

Howie staggered slowly to his feet, stunned by my insistence, by the fact that this was, indeed, the end. I was a little stunned myself; goodness knows I didn't want to lose him. My whole body ached to be back in his arms. But I knew I could never be with Howie again, not after what he'd done. No matter how much it hurt, it had to end.

My father was physically absent for most of my life, and yet he had managed to teach me how a man should act and what a man should be. My father never cheated on my mother and so that was my standard. A man should not cheat. I would not compromise.

Of course, now I see it wasn't only my high standards that made me so rock-solid in sending Howie on his way. There was, in that teenage girl, a self-protectiveness already at work, a belief that it was better to sever a relationship as soon as it became clear things weren't going to work out, rather than stay and risk the eviscerating pain of eventually being left behind. I think my teenage heart had already absorbed this painful belief: Men leave. Sometimes even when they don't want to.

CHAPTER TEN
College

After twelve years in predominantly white schools, I hoped, at the age of sixteen, to spend my college career surrounded by African Americans. I really, really wanted to attend a historically black school.

I dreamed about Clark and Virginia-Union. I fantasized about becoming a Spellman woman, walking proudly down the streets of Hotlanta on the arm of a Morehouse man. I sent away for applications to several of these schools, but one day before I finished filling them out Mommy woke me and said, "Come on, Yasah. Let's take a ride up to New Paltz."

We got in the car and headed up the New York State Thruway, across the gleaming Hudson River, past apple orchards and lush vineyards to the Catskills and this quaint little village and a pretty little campus of the State University of New York. I thought we were just checking it out as a backup school. But my mother climbed from the car and looked around and announced, in so many words, "Well, Yasah, how do you like your new school?"

It never occurred to me to question Mommy's decision. All my life I had this deep and abiding trust in my mother and her word. If she said to me "Ilyasah, jump over this stick," I would do it without hesitation because I knew she was leading me in the right direction. So when she said "Go to New Paltz," I said "Yes ma'am." Later I figured out she had somehow pulled some strings and gotten me into New Paltz without the usual application process.

Looking back now, I believe she sent me to New Paltz in part because that was what she could afford. The tuition there was considerably less than my high school tuition, and Mommy had six daughters to put through school.

But I also think she worried I'd be lost if she sent me south to a historically black college, or to some big university anywhere. I was young and sheltered, largely innocent of racial politics. I was completely unprepared to play the role people would want me to play as the daughter of an African American hero. I had not a clue who I was, either as the daughter of Malcolm X or as simply myself, Ilyasah Shabazz. Mommy probably worried that if I enrolled at a historically black college, the expectations she had so carefully and thoroughly shielded me from my entire life would rise up like a tidal wave and swallow me whole.

Of course, it happened anyway. Almost.

The State University of New Paltz was not exactly a "black" college in 1979. Of the more than six thousand undergraduate students, only about ten percent were African Americans or African. Still, that was hundreds of people of color, far more than had attended any school I had gone to. Walking onto campus that first summer I was ecstatic at the sight of so many beautiful faces of color: African Americans, Africans, Latinos, Native Americans, African Caribbeans. All of a sudden it didn't matter that New Paltz was not one of the schools of my dreams; I was just so happy to be at a school with people of color.

In my exuberance and naïveté I greeted every person of color, especially African Americans, I saw walking across the quad. My famous line was "Hi, my name is Ilyasah and I live in 302A Du Bois." I invited everyone to come visit and I meant it innocently and sincerely. I thought we were all one big family.

Certainly my new family had already begun exerting its influence, including embracing my full name, Ilyasah. Mommy, for reasons of her own, had set me up in a dorm called Crisspell. She took me out shopping for all the basic dorm room equipment, which I picked out myself: blanket and comforters for my bed, other linen, posters and hot pots and an eight-track clock radio.

Crisspell was a single-sex dorm and the girls in it were, for the most part, white. My roommate, whose name I can no longer remember, had a curly blonde Afro; she looked a bit like Little Orphan Annie. She was nice, from what I remember; all the girls in my suite were nice. But I barely got to know them because no sooner had my mother kissed me good-bye and departed than a group of older African American students decided I should be in the "black" dorm, named after W. E. B. Du Bois. These students knew who I was because a girl from Mount Vernon named Darlene, who used to hustle with us at my friend Tony's house, was now a student at New Paltz and had already spread the word. The group presented its decision to me as a fait accompli; they arrived, packed up my things, moved me down the hill to Du Bois. It never occurred to me that I had anything to say about this move. I was a tumbleweed blowing in the wind and that wind, usually provided by my mother, was now blowing from a different direction. My people wanted me. I smiled and tumbled along.

For the first time in my life I became MALCOLM X'S DAUGH-TER! Everywhere I went on campus, people already knew who I was or, at least, who they thought I should be. I'd be walking along the path, thinking about my next class, and suddenly someone I didn't know was right up in my face. "Are you Malcolm X's daughter?" It was demanded with such undisguised skepticism I felt like pulling out my ID to prove it to all concerned. "What are you doing here?" Other people would just point and whisper as I passed, their voices traveling on the wind. *There she goes! Are you certain that's Malcolm X's daughter? She sure doesn't look it!* It was startling and bewildering and a little disturbing. I was sixteen years old. What did they want from me?

What I knew about my father at this point in my life came not from what I'd read but from what was shared by Mommy and family friends. I knew about Malcolm the husband, Malcolm the father, Malcolm the friend, not Malcolm X the spokesman, the revolutionary, the icon. I knew he was a great man who had made significant contributions to people of the African diaspora and the world, but I didn't know precisely what those contributions were. I didn't know why some people were surprised to learn I was his daughter. I decided I needed to find out.

I had brought a copy of my father's autobiography with me from home. I sat down to read it, trying to distance myself from the man in its pages, trying not to think of him as my father but as simply a man.

Even so it was a very emotional experience. Although I'd lived with and played with the *Autobiography of Malcolm X* all my life, this was the first time I read it with anything approaching adult comprehension. The story of Malcolm Little's transformation into Malcolm X and then El-Hajj Malik El-Shabazz is one of the most powerful stories of the twentieth century. In some ways it is *the* story of the twentieth century, of the brutal oppression and degradation of one group of people by another and of that first group's fight to reliberate themselves physically, emotionally, and psychologically.

Night after night during those first summer months I sat in my dorm room reading and crying. My roommates must have thought I was losing my mind! But reading the story of Malcolm X filled me with awe for the man, for the human being he was. He was different from any man I had ever met or read about or saw on television, so honest and loyal and committed and genuine and deeply, deeply spiritual. Reading the *Autobiography* made me prouder than I already was to be the daughter of Malcolm X. But it also worried me. How in the world could I possibly ever live up to a man like that?

Much later in my life Attallah told me that all of us sisters called her during our freshman or sophomore years with questions about our identities. She always seemed to have the answers, to have the gift of knocking out our insecurities and uncertainties. "You don't owe an explanation to anyone," she said. "You are Malcolm X's daughter—you don't have to pass a test. You are his daughter and all he would want for you is to be whole as you explore yourself in this new space."

Still, that people expected me to be like my father was becoming quite clear. For one thing, I found myself running for cultural chairperson of the black student union. Somebody suggested it; someone else put my name on the ballot. A girl named Peaches wrote my campaign speech. She told me exactly what to say and how to say it and I stood up before the union and repeated her rhetoric word for word. I won.

Back in Du Bois, things started off well enough. My suite mates treated me nicely—so nicely that I was surprised, upon visiting the home of one of them over vacation, to find many of my clothes in her bedroom closet. Later I found out she had also been reading my diary when I was out of the room. And then I found out that several of them were talking about me behind my back, saying very hurtful things.

A friend of mine, named, appropriately enough, Ernest, took me aside one day toward the end of the first semester. "I think you should know," he said, not quite meeting my eyes. "People are saying things about you."

"Really?" I asked, not alarmed. I was unaccustomed to being the subject of rumors. Except for my dust-up with the Chain Gang, I had never encountered the kind of peer maliciousness and hostility that makes the lives of so many teenagers a living hell. Somehow I had slipped untouched through all three of my high schools, protected by Mommy, a compact circle of friends, and an impenetrable armor of guilelessness. It never occurred to me that people—black people, my people—would want to say bad things about me.

"You know Jessica?" Ernest asked.

Everybody knew Jessica. She was an upperclassman, a pretty girl, sandy-haired and voluptuous, the campus sexpot who had been around and around. Or so rumor had it.

"People are saying you're just like Jessica," Ernest said.

It turned out my friendly invitations to visit my dorm room had been misjudged. Badly misjudged. The talk was flying fast and furious that I was sleeping my way through freshman year, bedding down with anyone and everyone who walked through my door. My suite mates had done nothing to counter the rumors. They may even have begun them; I don't know.

Looking back from the advantage of adulthood, I can see that many of my young sisters and brothers were struggling themselves. They were away from home for the first time, thrust into a small-town, predominantly white environment when they were used to the neighborhoods of Brooklyn and Queens; some of them were unprepared for the academic challenges that lay ahead.

Then, too, I imagine some of the anger stemmed from their disappointment in me. They were expecting Malcolm X's daughter and what they got was a young girl educated in predominantly white schools who knew her African history but didn't seem to grasp the undercurrent of tension on campus between blacks and whites. I don't remember exactly how it happened, but I imagine a group of eager, excited students, self-styled revolutionaries all, marching over to Crisspell to liberate the progeny of *their hero*, the by-any-means-necessary man (though they may not have truly understood what he meant by that statement). I imagine them expecting a girl with flowing locks and a dashiki, expecting a girl with raised fists and burning eyes, expecting a fiery Black Muslim who came to shake up things in sleepy little white New Paltz. And they walk into the room and there I am, sitting on the bed in my little brown T-shirt with my name "Yasah" in tan letters across the front and my tan walking shorts and my cute little sandals and my relaxed hair in a ponytail. "Hi!"

Whoa.

Whatever the reasons for the wild rumors, I was so stunned and so hurt by them that I burst into tears. Poor Ernest didn't know what to do. He tried to comfort me and after awhile I calmed down and made my way back to my room.

I called my girlfriend Kristine. She was a senior at Hackley and we had often talked about her coming up to visit me at New Paltz on a school holiday. "You can't come here, Kristine," I said. "This is a whole different scene." Kristine was white and I didn't want her presence to aggravate what was already a bad situation. Maybe no one would have said anything, but I didn't want to take a chance.

And then, as usual, I turned to Mommy. During a visit home between semesters, I went out to dinner with Mommy and confided in her.

"People are saying all these things," I told her, tearing up. "They're saying I sleep with boys, I sleep with girls."

"Oh, baby," she said. Her voice sounded so sad.

"Mommy, I don't know why they're saying these things. But . . . I was wondering if I could move off campus?"

She didn't hesitate. "Of course."

I was surprised it was that easy. Yes? Just like that?

"Oh, thank you, Mommy. Thank you!" And I hugged her and gave her a big, fat kiss. She was so beautiful, my heroine then and always. Looking back now I realize my mother understood my sense of betrayal because she herself had been so bitterly betrayed.

She knew I was in pain and she knew she had to help, just the way she always did. She didn't ask how much it would cost or wonder aloud how she would afford it, and I, not thinking in those terms, didn't ask. At the end of my freshman year I moved into the South Side Terrace apartments, about half a mile from campus. One bedroom, a kitchen, dining and living room, bathroom, and a terrace just outside the sliding glass door. When Mommy came to visit my new home she took me out and bought me all new furniture.

Having experienced the **Autobiography,** I wanted to explore my father's life and work even more deeply, so I signed up for a class on Malcolm X. The instructor, a very young, very kind visiting professor from Morehouse, Dr. George Roberts, knew who I was without my telling him but was very kind in not making me stand out. The professor would occasionally ask me questions, but only in the way he asked other students. *Did you read the assignment? What was Marcus Garvey's influence on Malcolm X? From whom did Elijah Muhammad receive the mantle of leader of the Nation of Islam?* He never put me on the spot.

It was this professor who helped me really understand my father's philosophy and his enormous contribution to our people and to humankind. Again I was deeply moved by Malcolm X's lovingness, his selflessness. It was so beautiful. For the first time in my life I had experienced the lack of unity and self-love that has been so destructive to our people. To understand how hard my father worked to rid us of all that just blew me away.

One day the professor asked who in class would be ready for a revolution? All hands shot up, as did mine.

170

"That's good," he said. "But the next revolution will be waged not on horseback with shotguns but in these very chairs. The next revolution will be won by our people advancing themselves through education, through each of us taking seriously the responsibility to use what we learn here to attack social and economic injustice."

It was around this time that I first met my aunt Hilda. Hilda is my father's eldest sister, the second child and first girl born to Louise and Earl Little. In the *Autobiography* my father says Hilda was like a second mother to him in the years after his father's murder. She cooked and cleaned and attended to the younger children as their mother struggled to keep the family from falling apart. Although we had little contact with my father's brothers and sisters when I was a child, Mommy never discouraged our interest in that side of the family. When Attallah, at the age of seventeen or eighteen, wanted to reconnect, my mother gave her as much information as she could about the family's whereabouts. Attallah located Aunt Hilda in Massachusetts and went for a visit; she came back beaming with joy.

"She's wonderful, Ilyasah," Attallah said. "You really should meet her. You and she look just alike!"

When I got to college and began exploring my father's life, I telephoned Aunt Hilda. She was pleased to hear from me and promptly invited me to visit her in Massachusetts. I drove up one weekend with my friends Eliot and Danielle, excited and a little nervous about meeting this new relation. But Aunt Hilda put me immediately at ease, hugging me and welcoming me into her home.

171

"We do look alike," I told her, delighted. She was tall and strong-looking and brown-skinned just like I was. I thought she might be me in forty years.

"Actually," she said with a smile, "you look more like your aunt Yvonne."

We spent the whole weekend shopping and sightseeing around Boston and talking nonstop. One of the first things she told me was that she had dreamed about my father in those first, painful days after his assassination.

"He came to me and told me everything was okay where he was," Aunt Hilda told me. "He said, 'It's so peaceful here. There's not a worry in the world.' "

Hearing her story affirmed my belief that Daddy was in a better place and gave me an amazing sense of peace.

Aunt Hilda also told me her mother was deliberately and cruelly harassed into a state of nervous exhaustion and then stripped of her children and placed in a mental institution because a local probate judge coveted the family land. He put incredible pressure on Louise Little to sell, telling her she could receive welfare and still own the land. She refused to sell but that didn't stop him. He arranged for her monthly widow's support check to come through him, and every time she went to pick it up, he pressured her more. She was alone, without support, struggling to raise eight children, and eventually her physical health declined and the authorities pounced. Despite her education and intellect, Louise Little was a black woman alone in 1930s America; she had no defense against the power of white officials. On the day she was taken away, welfare officials came to the house and told her they would take her somewhere where she would be given food and clothing for the children. They promised to bring her back that afternoon, but she never returned to that house.

My grandmother Louise remained institutionalized until 1963, when her children, who had, despite it all, grown up and made good lives for themselves, managed to win her release. A cousin told me about that special day when Grandma Little came home.

"She was beautiful. Her thick, long silky hair was braided so neatly. She sat so peaceful, and almost motionless. The years of institutionalized, lonely self-talk had been her only reality."

Grandma Little lived for a time in Michigan with her son Wilfred and spent the last six years of her life cozily nestled in a house adjoining a small grocery store owned by her daughter Yvonne.

I never met my grandmother. She died in 1989, before I had fully reconnected with that side of the family. I attended her funeral with my mother, and sitting among my aunts, uncles, and cousins I knew Louise Little's strength and spirit were not crushed by the injustices inflicted upon her, but remained very much alive.

By the time I was a sophomore in college, Mommy's career at Medgar Evers College of the City University of New York had blossomed. She was appointed director of institutional advancement and was fully involved in raising money for scholarships, activities, and programs for the school.

Her influence beyond the school had also begun to spread. She served as a volunteer presidential adviser on human rights issues, race relations, and children's issues to Presidents Gerald Ford and Jimmy Carter, and would later do the same for President Bill Clinton. She traveled across the country speaking at high school and college graduation ceremonies, spreading the truth about Malcolm X and his message. She told the world her husband's primary goal was the economic, political, and social empowerment of African Americans. Nothing more, nothing less.

"Malcolm's agenda was human rights, international sisterhood and brotherhood, self-determination, and self-defense," she used to say.

Or, in my father's own words, "Why should White people be running all the stores in our community? Why should White people be running all the banks in our community? Why should the economy of our community be in the hands of the White man?

"Our people have to be made to see that any time you take your dollar out of your community and spend it in a community where you don't live, the community where you live will get poorer and poorer and the community where you spend will get richer and richer. Then you wonder why where you live is always a slum area."

Mommy was also active in so many social and political organizations it would make any other person exhausted just to think about it: the NAACP, the Coalition of 100 Black Women, the Links, Jack and Jill, and, of course, her sorority, Delta Sigma Theta, to name a few. Now that her daughters were all getting older and heading off on their own, she was beginning the worldwide travels that would take her to Brazil, Ghana, Kenya, South Africa, China, and other places in her continuing effort to improve the lives of struggling people everywhere.

But as busy as she was, Mommy always made her daughters priority one. And she found time to mentor and advise our friends and other African American women throughout the country. She developed a reputation for encouraging women, especially in their careers. She had begun the unofficial mentoring of hundreds of young women and she would continue this for the rest of her life. Here's an example: I remember once a young woman came to her, afraid and upset. She was pregnant and her mother, ashamed and angry, wanted to send her south to have the child. But the girl wanted desperately to stay in Westchester and finish high school. So my mother helped create a program that was geared toward helping pregnant teenagers finish their education instead of dropping out.

My mother's desire to give stemmed both from her own naturally generous heart, from Muslim duties, and from the pain she had experienced. If you're the kind of person Betty Shabazz was, once you've experienced suffering and know in your bones how much it hurts, you don't want to see anyone else go through the same thing. I think Mommy reached out so much because she had needed someone to do the same for her after Daddy was assassinated. She knew what it felt like to need someone to hug you and say "Everything's going to be all right."

That desire to give, to reach out, and reach back was present in me, too, even when I was unsure about the larger purpose and direction of my life. While in college I got a part-time job at the St. Cabrini Group Home for Girls, a lock-up facility in upstate New York. My first day there I met a beautiful little girl named Donna who was only twelve years old but had already been branded a delinquent. She reminded me of my little sister Malikah—big for her age but cute and innocent. As I watched, one of the counselors began ordering Donna around, speaking down to her and using very unkind words. One thing led to another and soon the two were rolling on the floor fighting. Donna got the best of the counselor in front of all the other girls for a while, but then he managed to pin her down (like she was one of the boys) and threw her into what they called "timeout"—a small, sparsely furnished room.

The counselor was furious. He called the nurse's office and asked for an injection to sedate Donna. But I couldn't bear the sight of a needle being injected into her and so I asked if I could talk to her first.

"Are you nuts? She's out of control! She's dangerous."

"Please," I said. I wasn't sure why but I felt that if I could talk to Donna, I could reach her.

"Fine," the counselor said and let me into the room. Donna was sitting on the floor crying. I hugged her and talked to her as one would talk to a child, which she was. Of course she didn't want that needle, just someone to talk to her, someone to listen, to treat her like the young girl she was instead of a number or a statistic. Or a monster they feared. After we talked for a while, Donna agreed to apologize to the counselor, wash her face, say a prayer, and go to bed.

I loved working at the facility. The girls learned to trust me, and we developed a great rapport because I treated them as Mommy treated me, with lots of love and direction. I used my Sears credit card to charge the girls a bunch of necessities: sneakers, sandals, pants, shorts, toiletries. They used to make all kinds of crafts for me to show their love. One girl, who was supposed to be so dangerous and mean, also won my heart. She had beautiful, dark Egyptian skin, but she did not seem proud of it. In fact, I figured the reason she probably seemed intimidating was because she had probably been teased all her life because of her dark complexion. I gave her lots of attention as well, and for my birthday she made me a hanging mobile of little pink heart-shaped pillows with pearls hanging on the invisible threads. I looked at it and marveled that it was made by someone who was supposed to be so unruly and tough.

One thing was clear: My purpose in life was not to be a great orator. Daddy's brilliance in that regard had not been passed down in the genes.

While still in college, I was invited to be one of the keynote speakers at a national Delta Sigma Theta convention. Just the idea made my stomach churn, but I could not turn them down; Mommy was a Delta and, besides, the theme of the talk was "Daughters of the Revolution," and it involved an antidrug message. I was supposed to appear alongside Martin Luther King Jr.'s daughter Bernice, Bishop Desmond Tutu's daughter Mpho, and Jesse Jackson's daughter Santita. But I took one look at the program and got on the phone with Mommy.

"I don't know if I can do this," I said.

"Yasah, you'll be fine. Just say what's in your heart."

What was in my heart? How did I know what was in my heart? And why would two thousand people want to hear that anyway? In the end, my mother wrote my speech, gave me some pointers on addressing an audience, and sent me on my way.

When I arrived early on the appointed day, the organizers greeted me warmly and ushered me to the stage, to my seat at a long table of people. I was introduced to the other speakers and tried to make chitchat through the dull roar of my own nervousness. A waiter appeared bearing a plate full of food. This was a breakfast conference of at least one thousand people, and all around me the auditorium was abuzz with the sound of forks meeting plates, but the idea of eating was way beyond me. I pushed my food around for a bit, then eased the plate out of my line of sight.

And then it was time for the program. One by one the speakers stood and approached the microphone. They all seemed so confident, so calm and collected. They spoke passionately about their hopes and dreams for the progress of African people everywhere. Ms. Tutu's speech stood out especially. She spoke about the bloodshed taking place in South Africa, about the centuries of violence and oppression still being waged against her people, and she connected that involuntary genocide with the choice of young African Americans to destroy themselves and their people by using and fighting over drugs. It was a powerful comparison and it made my head throb and my knees tremble. *How in the world was I going to follow that? What was I going to talk about that even came close to what she was saying?* I looked out over the sea of faces; they were waiting for inspiration and I didn't think I could deliver it. My father had said it all, and said it brilliantly. I was going to get up there and add . . . what?

Speech after speech, I sat in my chair getting sicker and sicker to my stomach. Finally, just before my turn arrived I leaned over to one of the organizers and whispered desperately, "I'm not feeling well!"

It was certainly true; I thought I was going to be sick right there on the podium.

"Horrible, horrible cramps," I whispered. "I'm afraid I can't make it. I need to go back to my room."

The woman nodded sympathetically and helped me off the podium. I slunk back to my room feeling a little embarrassed and greatly relieved. It would be many years before I was finally able to overcome the fear of public speaking. Not by becoming my father or mother, but by becoming myself.

Once ensconced in my South Side apartment I settled down to college life. Slowly I gathered a circle of friends—Emerald, Joy, Lanie, Sharon, Danielle, Felice, and Kim—who accepted me for who I was. The more radical students on campus, the ones who had hoped to singe New Paltz with a little Malcolm X fire, gradually came to realize I was not my father, and either accepted me as I was into their circle or left me alone.

But there were still occasional incidents. Once, as I was playing Pac Man in the student union building between classes, a brother came up as I was refreshing my lipstick and began to lecture me. He informed me that sisters were not supposed to wear lipstick, didn't I know that? Lipstick, he said, was full of swine, unsanitary, unhealthy, and a symptom of the brainwashing that had taught us all our natural colorings were not good enough. I was flabbergasted; all I wanted to do was put a little chocolate brown moisture on my lips. I went home and called Mommy to ask what she thought. Her response was pure Mommy: Don't let anyone dictate who you are or who you should be.

"Honey, if you want to wear lipstick," she said, "wear it in good health."

It was Mommy, and the grounding she had given us, that allowed me to climb into my lifeboat and ride the waves of expectations and dictations that came during those years. Part of college for any student is finding out who he or she is; for African American students, the quest can be especially difficult. For far too many of our young people, excelling academically is considered the opposite of being authentically black. And so they arrive at college and go to one extreme or the other, trying to prove themselves.

I was fortunate in that my mother raised us with such a solid grounding in African and African American history, such a love and appreciation for who we were and whence we came, that I never felt I had to prove myself to white people. And although I was initially taken aback by the young brother's comment about my lip gloss, I was not thrown by it into a tizzy of having to prove myself to black people either. Because deep inside I knew the color of my lipsticks or the style of my hair had no bearing on my legitimacy as a proud African American woman. In that regard, at least, I knew who I was.

And so I focused on going to class and doing what I had come to New Paltz to do. I was a math major and very serious about it, until I got to linear math and had no idea what language the professor was speaking. I switched to biology and plowed ahead. I didn't smoke, didn't party too hard, rose each morning and ran six miles for exercise.

During my third year at New Paltz I got a call from Mommy telling me to go to Pennsylvania and pick up Gamilah at Lincoln University. I don't remember the details, but I did as instructed and my sister came to live with me for a while and to take classes at

New Paltz. Later Malaak also came to live with me for a while after deciding she did not like life at Springfield American International College. For a while there I felt like the pit stop for my younger sisters. I took the responsibility seriously. Once, driving along Route 32, the main thoroughfare through campus, I saw Malaak walking along. I knew she was supposed to be in class, so I stopped the car and, just like Mommy, said, "Get in." Then I drove her to class and watched while she went inside.

Despite my harsh introduction to the social perils of college life, I ended up enjoying my time at New Paltz immensely. Moving off campus turned out to be a blessing in disguise, as it allowed me to meet and befriend slightly older people, such as a woman named LaVallis. LaVallis lived in the condo next to Tammy, another friend, and she would later come to help me greatly in a time of need.

After switching my major to biology, I worked hard to keep my grade point average at a decent level because I had plans for medical school—or, rather, Mommy had plans. She had it all worked out: I was going to graduate, go to medical school, become a doctor, get a condominium, get married, have a family. She was so rock-solid certain and she was Mommy, so who was I to contradict?

Besides, I felt as though the daughter of Malcolm X and Betty Shabazz should certainly be doing something important, something great. Being a doctor sounded about right, though I was not inherently interested in a career in medicine. But the expectations of my fellow students had not left me untouched. Clearly I wasn't going to be a campus radical. Clearly I wasn't a great orator like my father—Peaches could attest to that. I did not have all the answers, nor the unwavering confidence my mother seemed to possess. At least if I became a doctor I could dedicate my life to helping my people preserve and maintain their physical health. Maybe that's what Mommy thought, too.

But the best-laid plans of even someone as seemingly invincible as my mother can go astray. In 1984 an accident canceled my medical school plans.

I had graduated a few weeks before with Mommy and all of my sisters looking on. Attallah had made my dress for me, a fuchsia-and-white ruffled concoction that I thought was just the bomb. And I thought she was just the bomb for being able to sew like that! Having my sisters and Mommy around me that day was so very special. They all stayed at my apartment and we told stories and made gentle fun of Mommy and laughed and laughed and laughed.

I was now living in the historic town of Newburgh in a lovely old neighborhood full of huge prewar homes, arching trees, and picturesque views of the surrounding mountains. My apartment was part of a renovated schoolhouse; it was airy and spacious, with cathedral ceilings and high windows emphasizing the view outside. All in all, the apartment was a big step up from my place back in New Paltz.

I was in that heady, slightly surreal fissure of time that comes after college graduation, when all the doors of the world seem open, but only for a moment. The days of youthful exploring and testing are over. Now is the time to get serious, to get a job, choose a career. And once you choose, all the other doors now standing open will begin, one by one, to close.

I still had a few credits to earn before my graduation was official, so I was working at a department store while finishing up classes at New Paltz. One day my friend Lisa, who was now living in Washington, and a friend named John drove up from D.C. for the weekend. They arrived late Wednesday night. My friend Danielle came over and we all stayed up until the sunrise, talking and laughing with that untamed energy young people have for old friends. I managed to catch forty winks before going off to work.

After work I went to class, then back to my apartment. My friends were still there, still talking and laughing and now drinking. Though bone-tired, I agreed to go out with them. I suggested a nightclub called The Capricorn, but considering Lisa had driven her fancy car all the way from D.C., she wanted to drive down to the city. We went back and forth for a while, debating whether we shouldn't wait until the next day, a Friday, before going to New York. But Lisa was persuasive: The Capricorn was nice but small-town and its crowd was mostly white. The city would be more fun.

We drove down to New York and, after wandering around for a while, ended up at Studio 54. Once inside we noticed that something was slightly different about the crowd, but we couldn't put our finger on it, until one of us realized there were almost no women in sight. A gay party was being held. We stayed at the disco for a little while and then decided to head home. I was so sleepy I could barely keep my eyes open, but because the others had been drinking and I had not, they all piled into the backseat.

"I'm too tired to drive," I told them, but nobody listened. Their heads were swimming and they knew they couldn't steer themselves, let alone a car. So, after a few minutes, I climbed into the driver's seat.

The rest of the night is spotty, as these things often are. I remember being on Interstate 87 and saying again how incredibly sleepy I was. The next thing I knew, I was waking up in the hospital.

The truck driver who stopped to help us and who called the police said we were speeding up I-87 when the car veered to the left, struck a rail, and bounced back to the right of the road. We hit a tree, overturned, and tumbled fifteen or twenty feet down an embankment.

I was in a coma for three days. When I woke up the first time I saw Attallah standing at the side of my bed. She had brought pictures of my graduation and she showed them to me. Mommy, who was outside instructing the nurses, came into the room when she heard I was awake. I felt so happy seeing my mother and my sister I wanted to smile, but all I could do was float. There was no pain that I can remember; I felt happy and giddy and sleepy. Then I went back out.

The next time I woke up I heard Mommy speaking to someone—a nurse, a doctor—in that forceful, commanding way of hers. She was asking a question or giving instructions, something, and the sound of her voice filled me with happiness. I felt completely safe. Mommy was there and she was in control. I closed my eyes and drifted off again.

When I finally woke up for good I was grateful to be alive and all in one piece. It took awhile before anyone told me what had happened to the others. John and Lisa were in the same hospital, injured, but would recover fully in time. Danielle was a different story.

She had been taken to a hospital in New York City. The accident had severely traumatized her spinal column; the doctors told her she would be paralyzed.

I cannot imagine that moment for Danielle. This information hit me like a punch to the stomach and I cried for my beautiful friend. After getting out of the hospital, John drove back up to New York and he and Lisa and I went to visit Danielle. She was in the hospital, on her back in her room, unable to move. Seeing her that way was devastating. In the years to come Danielle, who loved to dance, to feel her body moving through space, would struggle to adjust to her new reality.

For weeks as I lay in the hospital recuperating, I had no idea what I looked like. But I began to suspect it was bad when Gamilah came to see me. She took one look and burst into hysterical tears. All I could do was laugh and tell her, "It's okay, Gamilah. I'm fine."

But she just started screaming. Mommy had to come and take her out of the room to calm her down.

After I was moved from the intensive care unit into a regular room with Lisa, I noticed, too, that my friends who came to visit would not look at me. They would spend most of their time talking to Lisa and direct only a few comments my way. But then my friend and old science partner Sue came to visit. She pulled up a chair and sat right next to my bed, pulling books and knitting needles and yarn from her bag. Later I realized what a good friend she really was.

When I was finally able to get out of bed and look in a mirror, I was shocked. The whole right side of my face had been smashed in during the accident. There were open lacerations on my cheek, and my nose and forehead were purple and black and swollen and cut. My eye was bloodred. All in all, it was a gruesome sight.

I remained in the hospital for about two months and it took several more months after that for all the physical scars to heal. During

185

those months it was painful to see how people reacted; it gave me a small insight into the way a physically disabled or deformed person is treated by the world, how brave they must be to go out and face society each day. Once I was shopping in a store and saw a woman for whom I had modeled occasionally. My face and neck were still bandaged and I must have looked quite a sight. As I walked toward this woman—I'll call her Jane—to say hello, she turned a corner in the store and disappeared. I continued shopping and saw Jane again; again she escaped. Finally, as I was leaving, I caught up with her near the door.

"Jane!" I cried, happy to see her, thinking she would be happy to see me. It was a small town and I knew she knew what had happened.

But Jane turned green and backed away. "Ilyasah! I'm sorry, so sorry," she said over and over. She couldn't get away fast enough and as she left, she would not look me in the face.

A few weeks later a friend and I went down to the disco Bentley's for a night out. I asked a guy if he wanted to dance. He took one look, said no, and backed up like I was a monster.

Mommy, of course, wanted me to come home. But my friend LaVallis, who had a large condo in Fishkill, invited me to move in with her and I accepted. LaVallis was wonderful during those months, escorting me to the hospital for my physical therapy and checkups and generally helping me back to my feet.

In the aftermath of the accident, I would sometimes lie awake at night, praising God and wondering why my life had been spared. I know there's no way I should have lived through that; it was far too violent a collision. Danielle and I would talk about trying to find the meaning behind the whole thing.

As the years passed and life went on, I put the accident behind me. And it wasn't until my mother passed that the reason God spared my life that night on Interstate 87 dawned on me. For one thing, I know if something had happened to me, my mother would have been devastated. She had already suffered so much painful grief in her life; how could she have handled the horror of losing a child?

Then, too, I believe God knew there would come a day when Mommy would finally need someone to take care of her, when the woman who had dedicated her life to helping not only her daughters but countless people of all cultures and colors would need help herself. And when someone would be required to fill, in some small measure, Mommy's shoes when it was finally time for her to go on and meet her husband.

CHAPTER ELEVEN

Daddy's Home

L ife was a whirlwind after the accident as my body and soul recuperated from the trauma and my heart pressed onward, trying to find its way in the world.

My friend LaVallis, in whose condo I'd lived during my recuperation, got married. Mommy drove up from Mount Vernon and mothered us all, preparing LaVallis for her special day with spa treatments and hairstyling advice and copious amounts of love. After that, I found a new roommate, Tammy, and together we moved into a town house in Wappingers Falls, a small, Hudson River town that would, a few years later, be made infamous by Tawana Brawley.

With medical school on hold, I decided it was time to look for work. I applied for a job at Ciba Geigy, a large pharmaceutical company. It was one of my first job interviews and I thought I was handling it pretty well, until the interviewer asked, "What are some of your strengths?"

I didn't realize this was standard interview-speak and that I was supposed to say something like "I'm highly motivated" or "I love to work!" Instead I thought for a moment then said, "Well, as you know, by nature all black women are strong."

I did not get that job.

For a while I worked as a substitute teacher at Mount Vernon High School. Walking into the school the first time was a shock for me: the lack of supplies, the absence of books, the low expectations, and the air of ennui. Some days I was told to just go into a classroom and turn on a video. But I found the children were as hungry to learn as anywhere—if you could make the learning interesting and relevant to them.

Once, when the topic of the day was essay-writing, I began by asking the students who their favorite recording artists were. Then I asked if there was one place they could go, where would it be? And how would they travel—boat, airplane—and what would they do when they arrived? And what is their biggest dream?

This was a classroom of struggling students and people had warned me it would be difficult to get them to simply settle down and be quiet, let alone learn. But in this case they were all interested. They scribbled down the answers on pieces of paper I had distributed to them while I wrote on the board.

"Now," I said, when they had finished. "I want you to write me an essay using all the things we just wrote down. You went to sleep, you had a dream, and . . ."

The results may not have been ready for publication in *The New Yorker*, but they were passionate and heartfelt and clear.

Meanwhile my baby sister Malikah had grown up and was living the life down in New York City. She was in the mix, knew everybody, and was forever getting tickets to this concert or passes to that hot event. Her life seemed very exciting, so I decided to move back to civilization and join in the fun.

I moved to Brooklyn, and once again, Mommy stepped in. She helped me get a job in the office of academic affairs at City University of New York. My work there, which I enjoyed, was helping to create and manage programs to encourage students who had dropped out of high school to pursue higher education.

Although I majored in biology in college, my real passion was in the arts. I had dabbled in theater as a child and while in college, but I never got seriously involved. I think if Mommy had not been so certain I should become a doctor I might have decided at an earlier age to pursue acting or music as a career.

As it was my short-but-sweet foray into the arts came after I graduated college and was casting about for meaningful and enjoyable work. When I told Mommy I wanted to give acting a try, she telephoned her friend Norman Jewison, the Canadian director known for his films *In the Heat of the Night*, *Moonstruck*, and *The Hurricane*, among others. Mr. Jewison in turn called a few people and the next thing I knew I was trying out for every soap opera on television. I managed to land bit parts, most of them nonspeaking, on "One Life to Live" and "All My Children." I even took lessons from an acting coach for a brief time, but in the end things didn't work out. I was far too inhibited back then to be a good actor.

Around that same time I met Spike Lee. I had gone to see his smash debut movie *She's Gotta Have It* and was surprised and pleased to see, at the end, various quotes from my father. I said to myself, "I want to meet this director."

I contacted Spike, who was gracious and welcoming. We became friends and he introduced me to the film world, giving me a job as a production assistant on his Michael Jordan commercials and even casting me in bit parts in some of his movies. But don't look for me in *Jungle Fever* or *School Daze*—all of my scenes ended up on the cutting room floor.

After awhile Spike was like family. But as much as I liked him, he could sometimes make me feel a little self-conscious. I was still young, still trying to figure out who I was supposed to be, and sometimes Spike did not make that easy. I had just moved down to the city after years in mostly white upstate New York, and I was into Madonna and the GoGos as much as the emerging hip-hop scene. When Spike invited me to a Knicks game, I got all dressed up in black ski pants, my favorite cable knit sweater, and what I thought were kicking boots: ivory, rugged, with an artillery chain around the ankles. Spike takes me to Madison Square Garden, sits me down, checks me out, and says, "So, you're into Madonna?" From the tone of his voice and the look on his face I knew it wasn't an idle question. I went home and gave the boots to my girl-friend Kathy. Spike also questioned my decision to relax my hair, saying he didn't think my father would like the idea.

That threw me for a loop. His comments came at a point when I was already thinking of cutting off my hair and starting from scratch, growing it out and then locing it—not necessarily because I wanted it that way but because it seemed the thing to do. But then I thought of my mother. Anyone who would suggest Betty Shabazz was not a proud, self-actualized, and fully committed African American woman would be laughed out of the room by anyone who knew her. Mommy's words—"Yasah, focus on yourself"—came back to me. Meaning: Whatever you want to do, do it, as long as you can look yourself in the mirror and know you're living the way God wants you to. All this other stuff really doesn't matter. So I decided to keep my hair relaxed.

One night I went to a Bobby Brown and Al B Sure concert, both of whom were friends of mine. I went with a guy who was a member of the group Najee. This guy knew everybody, all the other band members and production people, and it was a great time. We met an agent named Stephen Sands who worked at the William Morris Agency. He told me, "You need to come work with me."

I became his assistant, his right-hand woman. Together we sought new talent, booked shows, arranged tours, listened to music of all kinds in search of the next big thing. It was a great job, lots of fun, but it was a fast life of parties and concerts and receptions, and eventually Stephen decided it was *too* fast for him. He resigned to go to medical school and another agent, Leon Saunders, was hired to replace him. When Leon started asking me to get people on the phone for him and bring him coffee, I realized his idea of an assistant was very different from Stephen's. And from mine.

After leaving William Morris, I worked for Pendulum Records as coordinator of promotions and marketing. This was during the time when Digable Planets, Lisa Lisa of Cult Jam, and Lords of the Underground were all hot. But the two visitors who caused the most excitement among the women in the office were singer Christopher Williams, with whom I went out on a single, friendly date, and Fabrice Morvan, one half of the pop group Milli Vanilli. Everybody loved Fab. He was one fine African French brother.

It was during this time that I visited my father's grave for the first time in my life. I don't know what it was that prompted me; it just seemed the right time to go. Although Daddy was buried not twenty miles from our home in Mount Vernon, Mommy had never taken us to his grave when we were children. I'm not even sure if she ever went herself. Certainly she never mentioned it, and when I brought the idea up tentatively, she didn't really want to talk about it. It was simply too painful a place for her. Even decades after my father's death, the wound remained open for Mommy. She simply could not emotionally afford to look upon that site.

But I suddenly wanted to see it. So one day after work I got into my car, got on the Thruway, and headed north. It was the height of rush hour, and traffic was the usual New York mess. By the time I found the cemetery in Hartsdale the sun was setting and the gates were about to close.

I had no idea where to look, no idea even where to begin. Should I go left or right? Should I keep driving or just park and start looking around? It wasn't a small cemetery and there was no one around to ask. Dusk was rushing in and soon I would have to leave. What if I couldn't find Daddy? What if he wasn't really there at all?

Jittery with panic, I parked the car and leapt out. I walked and walked and walked until, suddenly, somehow, there it was. A simple, elegant brass plate, flat on the ground and inscribed:

HAJJ MALIK EL-SHABAZZ

MALCOLM X

1925–1965

Seeing his name on the tombstone filled me with such a sense of hollowness my arms began to ache. My head swam and my knees weakened; I wanted to just curl up right there on the ground beside him. Instead I cried. I cried torrents, and talked to him, calling his name, telling him how much I missed him, how sorry I was he had to go.

And then one of the cemetery caretakers drove past and told me the gates would be closing soon and it was time to go. I kicked myself for not bringing something to leave behind for my father, for Daddy. Some symbol of my love. I searched my pockets and my purse for something personal, something of me, but came up empty. In the end I removed the barrette from my hair and placed it gently inside the vase, the scheaf.

Shortly after that day I flew to Atlanta to meet with Dexter King. I wanted to talk with him about the King Center and its functioning; I thought my father deserved something similar, a living memorial to his life and his work. This was before Columbia University touched off a firestorm with its plans to tear down the Audubon and build a biotechnology research center on the site. Mommy was pulled into the maelstrom with university officials, city politicians, and community activists all tugging at her sleeve. Eventually Mommy gave the university her support for the medical center on two conditions: they create a permanent memorial on the site and a living memorial, providing medical scholarships to the young people of Harlem or other students in need, especially those who would commit to returning to their home communities to practice medicine.

Although there have been some bumps in the road, we are now on track toward making the site a vibrant, community-based educational and political center in my father's honor. I think Mommy, who for years had been unable to walk past the Audubon but eventually came to the point where she was looking forward to working there after her retirement, would be pleased.

I was still working at William Morris when Spike Lee first spoke to me about making a movie based upon my father's life. He was not the first person with the idea. Since producer Marvin Worth secured the film rights to my father's story in 1968 and made a documentary on the subject, writers as varied as James Baldwin, David Bradley, David Mamet, and Charles Fuller have tried their hands at writing a screenplay for a feature film. Billy Dee Williams expressed interest in playing the role. So did Richard Pryor. Sidney Lumet considered directing such a film, and Norman Jewison had actually gotten the go-ahead from Hollywood. Then Spike got wind of it.

Spike told me that a white man had no business directing a film about Malcolm X. He believed only a black man would be able to do my father's story justice and he vowed to wage a protest campaign to wrest control of the film from Jewison.

I don't know if Mommy had an opinion on this. She didn't participate in the discussion and neither did I. I liked and admired both Norman and Spike, and when Norman agreed to bow out of the picture I was like, oh, okay.

Spike invited me to try out for a part in the movie as my father's secretary. I wanted badly to play Laura, my father's sweet, lindy-hopping dance partner in his early days in Boston. Although I read for both parts, I landed neither. But at least this time I did make it onto the screen.

You can see me squeezing down the left aisle in a mosque as my father speaks, bringing converts to Islam. You can also see me when he steps outside of a mosque in one scene and is surrounded by well-wishers.

Being on the set of the movie was both exhilarating and awkward. Watching scene after scene of my parents' lives unfold felt slightly surreal. Denzel Washington was wonderful; he captured the essence of my father. But as much as I admired his work in movies such as *Glory* and loved the fact that he was a fellow Mount Vernonite, he was so clearly *not* my father that it was sometimes difficult to watch him work. Plus I was taller than Denzel. That felt strange because my father was so very tall—six feet, five inches—and always loomed even taller in my mind.

I'm not sure how many people on the set realized who I was. Certainly Spike knew, as did Denzel and Angela Bassett, who played Mommy. I thought she was a good choice to play Mommy, because she shared the same intelligence, beauty, grace, and elegance. She asked me questions about my mother and I answered as best I could. I told her how pleased my mother was to know she was portraying her.

The movie premiered in November 1992 at the world-famous Ziegfeld movie theater in midtown Manhattan. My friend Julie, who lived in my apartment building, had hired a car, but Mommy said, "Julie, you get in this car with us." At the premiere Mommy introduced Julie as her cousin—she had a way of making everyone feel special.

It was at the premiere that I first met many of the Little family members, including Aunt Yvonne and her daughter Debbie. As fate would have it, we met in the ladies' room. I took one look at these women and they looked at me and we knew instantly that we were related, although we had never seen one another before. We hugged and squealed and sat in the lounge for a while, chatting about our lives. I was amazed that they were strong, proud, up-standing, smart, and attractive relatives, because I had been relying on the *Autobiography*'s description of the Little family.

Mommy was very quiet during the movie itself. At several points she put her hands up, as if blocking something, some emotion, some memory she had not experienced in a while. Afterward she was smiling and gracious as people swarmed around her, offering congratulations. But in the car driving home she laid quietly against my chest.

And so the big question: What do I think of the movie? My an-swer is that I think Spike did a great job artistically. He made a long movie (more than three hours) intriguing and entertaining enough to hold the audience's attention. He was true to the details of my father's life as presented in the *Autobiography of Malcolm X* and in the screenplay by James Baldwin on which the movie was based.

But I don't think Spike really managed to capture the true depth of my father's life and work. If I could change one thing about the movie I would give more prominence to his words, his thoughts, his revolutionary vision for Africans all over the world. I would show how much he contributed to ending the physical, legal, and, more important, mental and spiritual oppression of our people. In *X* you saw that Malcolm X was a great, great man. But you didn't see why.

One other good thing came out of the movie for me: At the audi-tion I met a man who would become my first manager and then my boyfriend. Kedar Massenburg was charming, intelligent, and very smooth. He had a cell phone—this was the early 1990s, before everyone had one—and he kept whipping it out to make important business calls. He was a Muslim. He had just graduated from law school and was running a multifaceted entertainment business out of his four-story home. He had a fully outfitted studio in the basement and everything was just hooked up.

I needed a manager because a friend of mine, Julie Bearden, had helped me land a record deal at East West Records. I was going to try my hand at recording freestyle, hip-hop poetry about science and knowledge and identity. My sister Gamilah joined me and we called ourselves Shabazz by Birth.

But before we could actually complete our studio sessions, Gamilah performed on the "Arsenio Hall Show" as a cameo with Big Daddy Kane and went off and left me in the wind.

I might have pursued the recording solo but after Kedar became my manager and then my boyfriend, he persuaded me to drop the idea. He basically said, "No, that's not what you're going to do." He didn't think it was appropriate, and I acquiesced. In the end, things didn't work out with Kedar, so we parted as friends and went our separate ways. Today he is chairman and CEO of the legendary Motown Record Company.

A little later I met Jerrod at a social event in Washington, D.C. I was writing down my phone number for someone when a voice behind me said, "Can I have a copy of that?"

I turned around to see this gorgeous brother who stood seven feet one inch tall. I thought to myself, *Now that's more like it!*

We had a couple of dates. He told me he sold T-shirts for a living. *Honest work,* I thought. *But maybe I can help him find something more productive to do with his life.* Then he invited me to fly down to

Washington to attend some fund-raising affair his parents were involved in, and met me at the airport in the biggest Mercedes I had ever seen.

"You must sell a lot of T-shirts," I said.

"Well, to tell the truth," he said. "I play basketball for the Phoenix Suns."

I introduced him to Mommy, who was wary at first because she knew how professional athletes could be. But Jerrod was not a typical b-ball player. He was a deeply intelligent man who loved reading and who seemed to be spiritually connected as a Muslim. He had attended American University.

We fell head over heels in love. He kept encouraging me to move out to Phoenix, and after about eight months of dating, I finally agreed. I packed up my life in New York (still keeping my apartment just in case) and got on the plane with dreams of marriage in my head. I thought Jerrod and I would fly off together into the Arizona sun.

Looking back, that time of my life seems like one long, frolicking movie. The parties, the concerts, the expensive trips and expensive cars. Jerrod and I had a lot of fun together and got along so well we started an entertainment business with him as president and me as vice president. I see now that to him the business was mostly like a toy he bought to keep his girlfriend interested. I, on the other hand, was serious. I had written a hip-hop musical and we planned to produce it and take it on the road. We signed several up-and-coming artists and planned to use them in the show. We were going to make a record, recording and producing it ourselves. We had the studio and the money. We were going to be big.

But a few months after moving to Phoenix I found out Jerrod was not being faithful to me. Not only that, but the woman he was seeing turned out to be the daughter of Elijah Muhammad! She even told Jerrod her mother was, at one time, planning to marry my father, a story that turned out to be partly true. When my father decided he needed to be married to best continue his work as a minister of the Nation of Islam, he considered several young Nation of Islam sisters and even got engaged to one of them, this woman's mother. But then he met Mommy and there was no one else for him after that. Between Malcolm and Betty it was love.

But not, apparently, between Jerrod and me; at least not the kind of love I wanted for my life. I was devastated and so stunned I barely knew what to do. I went into a holding pattern. Not wanting to just throw away all the time and effort I had put into building the business, I moved out of Jerrod's bedroom into my own room upstairs and tried to carry on.

Eventually it was all just too strange and I gave up on the business and left Phoenix. Back home in New York, I crawled into my apartment and stayed there for weeks, not working, not dating, just being depressed.

One day Mommy came over and dragged me out of the house. In the back of the car in which we were riding she said, "Yasah, I have something for you."

She put a ring on my hand, a diamond ring. It was so beautiful I gasped. And I realized she was trying to tell me I had to be more important to myself than any man could ever be. And that a mother's love was more powerful and more enduring than any romantic love I would ever know.

Two days later I got up, got dressed, went out, and landed myself a job at Boardman in Greenwich, Connecticut.

That time in my life taught me a lot about the behavior of men. Before Jerrod, if I found out a man I was dating was cheating on me, I immediately ended the relationship and never spoke to him again. I thought cheating was a monstrous aberration. I didn't understand it at all.

But in Phoenix, surrounded by Jerrod and his friends, I came to believe that all men cheated. Professional athletes are not typical, of course; they live in a hypermasculine world where women are constantly throwing themselves at their feet. But watching their behavior I grew to believe that although they might be extreme, they were representative. Even guys who seemed so good, so decent as they drove to church with their families every Sunday, on Monday would be making a pass. Seeing this I said to myself, oh, I see. Men cheat. Okay.

But then I remembered my father, who never cheated on my mother, and even in the years immediately before marrying her lived a life of integrity and self-discipline. I realized that even if most men cheat, not all of them do. So what matters is not a man's looks or his job or the size of his wallet, but his values and goals. My father was an exception, yes. But where there is one exception there can be another. All I had to do was not compromise.

As for the women who tolerated that kind of behavior, I often wondered why they did it. I finally asked one woman I knew, who was dating a notoriously philandering player. She told me she was honored someone like him wanted someone like her, even if it was only part-time. After all, he could only be interested in that ultimate prize of the black professional athlete: a blue-eyed blonde.

"Most of these players want anything but a black girl," she said. "Especially if you're not light."

Statements like that are so sad I scarcely know where to begin addressing them. But this much I do know: Although I am (proudly) honey brown like my mother, I never felt unattractive while I lived in Phoenix. In fact, I had players coming on to me all the time, even though they knew I was dating Jerrod. I think that's because deep down inside men respect a woman who views herself as the prize, not as the competitor. And you have to draw the line, to make clear what kind of behavior you will and will not accept. If a woman compromises her values just to hang on to a man, she won't win his respect. More important, she won't win her own.

After I returned home from Phoenix, my mother and I grew closer than ever. Then two events occurred that changed the nature of our relationship. For the first time in my life, I stood up before an audience and spoke without fear of disappointing expectations.

And then Mommy got sick.

Growing Up X

The National Political Congress of Black Women planned to honor Mommy, Myrlie Evers-Williams, and Coretta Scott King—"The Three Ms," the widows of Malcolm, Medgar, and Martin—at its annual brunch. Someone from the organization called Attallah to ask if she would speak during the ceremony. Attallah couldn't do it, so she telephoned me.

Had it been anything else I would have said "No. Sorry, can't do it." I was more than a decade out of college by this time, but the fear of speaking in public, of being held to mountain-high expectations, still held me in its grip. Since sneaking off the stage at the Delta convention, I had avoided, to the best of my ability, any circumstances in which hundreds of people would sit in a room and hang on my every word.

But this was different. This was an event being held to honor Mommy, the most important person in my life and a woman I firmly believed deserved to be honored in her own right. How could I refuse a chance to stand up and tell the world what an amazing woman she was? How could I let pass a chance to publically thank her for all she had done?

So I agreed to speak. I decided not to tell Mommy, wanting to surprise her, and the organizers agreed to keep my secret. Finally the day arrived. My friend Kathy accompanied me to the ballroom in Washington, where we were greeted and taken into a special room to wait.

When it was time for all of us to take our seats on the stage, I walked over to where Mommy was sitting and surprised her. "Hey, Mommy!" She gave a little squeal of delight and hugged me before I went to my seat at the other end of the long table. There were the usual welcoming speeches and acknowledgments of guests. Then the program moved on to the unveiling of a specially commissioned painting that depicted the faces of my mother, Mrs. King, and Mrs. Evers-Williams, all overlooking a grand and glorious tree. Everyone applauded and posed for photographs. I sat next to Bernice King, feeling my heart speed up and my fingers tingle. But it was from excitement, not fear.

This time I was first up. I heard Eleanor Holmes Norton telling the guests of honor that the day was special not only because of them, but because it was their own daughters who would do the honoring. As I walked to the podium I saw that Mommy had jumped up from her chair and was also approaching the microphone. It made me smile. I don't know whether she was worried I'd fall apart or that she just wanted to give me a hug. But deep down inside I think she was just being Mommy—watching out for everyone, carrying the load for everyone, backing us all up because she knew we might not be able to make it alone.

But this time I didn't need my mother to speak for me. I knew what to say and how to say it; I could stand on my own as the living representative of all my mother's hard work and sacrifice. I could show the world that my sisters and I, fully realized human beings, were my mother's greatest accomplishments. I wrapped my arm around Mommy's shoulders and took the microphone without nervousness or fear.

I began by paying my respects to Mrs. King and Mrs. Evers-Williams, acknowledging their perseverance and triumphs over so many obstacles. I finally understood their collective pain and courage because I finally understood how hard Mommy's own struggle must have been. Then I told the audience how much I admired my mother for all she had accomplished against nearly overwhelming odds. I told them all she had done for her six daughters and for the world. I told them she was my role model, past, present, and future.

I told the story of how once, when I was about seventeen and Malaak was fourteen, we were driving on the parkway in Westchester County when Malaak announced she had to use the rest room. I pulled into the first available place, which happened to be a very fancy and expensive restaurant.

"I can't go in there," Malaak said.

"When in doubt, think of Mommy," I said, taking her hand.

I told the audience that Malaak and I marched into that restaurant like we owned it. We greeted all the folk going in and all the folk coming out and no one said a thing because we projected such self-confidence. Perseverance and self-respect. That's what I learned from my mother.

Then I told this story:

"As an adolescent I would say to her, 'Mommy, you're the most important person in my life.' And she would say, 'Ilyasah, you are the most important person in your life. Focus on yourself.'

"At the time I didn't understand, but now that I'm an adult, I do," I said. "And so I say, thank you, Mommy. And still, you are the most important person in my life."

At the end of my speech Mommy hugged me and I could feel through the embrace how moved she was. I returned to my seat and she took the microphone. Wiping away tears, she told the audience how surprised and pleased she was to have me there.

"But," she joked, "I have a few words for the honorable C. De-Lores Tucker afterward."

Then, slowly, deliberately, she began a story that was not part of her prepared remarks. She told of a little two-year-old girl whose father would come home late at night, grab a plateful of oatmeal cookies in one hand and her in the other, and go watch the evening news. It was, Mommy said, that girl's favorite part of the day and she looked forward to it with all the joy in her young heart.

It was a sweet memory, one I had heard so many times before that I had made it my own. But then Mommy went on to tell another part of the story, a part I had never heard before.

"When my husband was assassinated," Mommy said, "every car that passed, Ilyasah would get on the chair and look out the window. The car wouldn't stop. She would kick the door and go back to bed and go back to sleep."

After a pause, she went on. "And I didn't know how you explain to a little two-year-old about death. So what I began to do was, I'd take a cookie and break it in half and put it on a plate near the door. And she would come and get that. She would still look, but at least she'd be a little happier."

Listening to this story filled me with emotion—pride in my mother, sadness at her sorrow, grief at our collective loss. I thought of my father and how different life would have been for us had he lived. Not only for Mommy, but for my sisters and me and my nephew Malcolm. And for the world.

With a tissue from Dr. Tucker, Mommy dabbed at her eyes and said she had never talked to me about my feelings surrounding Daddy's death. Sounding as if she were speaking more to herself than to the hundreds of people in the room, Mommy said, "I still don't know how she feels."

Then she took a deep breath and looked out. "But today, I'm delighted to see that on her own she has learned about life and death." She looked over the long line of people toward me. I smiled my biggest smile.

"Standing here today I am delighted that she at least appears healthy," Mommy said.

And then she laughed.

That was a very important day in my life. After that day, my mother saw me in a new and different way: not simply as her daughter, a child who still needed the shelter and protection of her mother's arms, but as an adult, a woman on whom she herself could lean.

That was no small adjustment for Mommy to make. Since the day she watched her husband fall, my mother had driven herself relentlessly on our behalf. And although she was blessed with many dear friends who came to our rescue time and time again, Mommy knew that at the end of the day, it all came down to her.

Once, in a speech, she said, "You see, I am not for women having typical female roles. I had to do everything. I was the head of the household. When my husband lived, there was a role I played. When he was assassinated, I had to do everything. If I didn't make the money and bring the food in and pay the mortgage and pay the car note, and pay the school bill, we didn't eat, we didn't sleep, we didn't have a house. So I am not for women having specific roles and not doing what they should do, ought to do, and can do. Maybe if my life had been different I would say that women should not be in politics, that they should be in the home caring for their families. But my experience has not been that. I no longer believe that."

Mommy had pulled the load alone for so long, it was hard for her to scoot aside and let someone grab hold of the rope. But after my speech before the National Political Congress I detected a change in the way my mother viewed me. We had always been close, but after that day, we truly became best friends. She opened up to me in ways she had not before and talked, really talked, about my father and what he had meant to her as a woman and a wife. She told me about his discipline and all the work he did and his incredible commitment to his family and his people. She said something like, "Just because my husband taught me to love who I am doesn't mean he did anything wrong!" Meaning why in the world should people try to vilify a man who simply helped her become more in tune with herself and helped a people know and love their heritage?

Sometimes as she was drifting off to sleep or when she was really sad, she would talk to him. She would say, "Malcolm, Malcolm, why did you have to go?"

Once, when we were talking about men, I jokingly said,

"Mommy, how could you know what it's like out here? You had the best man in the whole, wide world."

"No, sweetheart," she said. "I had DE best man."

Sometimes she would just bask in the glory of the time she had with her husband; other times she couldn't talk about it because it became too painful. With my mother, it was almost as if her husband was assassinated yesterday.

Mommy also let me in on the astonishing extent of her activities. I found out about all the projects she was involved in, the dozens upon dozens of young women she was mentoring, the hundreds of people for whom she bought diapers or made strategic phone calls or dropped a check in the mail to help with tuition. I sat in my mother's office and heard the telephone ring over and over with requests. More than once I remember looking at her and she looked as though she was simply exhausted. Depleted in a way. But when she saw me looking she would smile and sit up straight and dive back into whatever that day held for her. Sometimes I would tell her, "Mommy, you're doing too much. Sometimes you have to say no."

But Mommy rarely said no. "Yasah, charity is just one of the things you do in life. Just like you have to drink water, you have to give back."

I'm not sure whether it was my mother's growing confidence in me or simply a by-product of growing up, getting older, and becoming more grounded, but during this time I began discovering who I was and what my purpose was in this life.

My new understanding of my place in the universe didn't

happen in a flash. I did not have a revelation or wake up one morning with the nagging issue of my life suddenly resolved. But gradually, bit by bit, I began to understand that I didn't have to shoulder those expectations first foisted upon me in my teenage years.

I realized that I didn't have to re-create the amazing lives of my mother or my father; all I had to do was be my own best self. I came to understand that as long as I was a good person, as long as I lived by the values instilled in me by my parents and incorporated God's will into my life, I was just fine.

It may sound simplistic, but the simple truths are usually the most profound.

I learned one more thing during this time. I learned that Mommy, for all her amazing strength and perseverance, was not invincible.

Recovery

S ometime in the late fall and early winter of 1995–96, friends started calling me to ask about my mother's health. Mommy had recently returned from attending the International Women's Conference in Beijing, China, and several people who saw her going out or coming back said they were worried about how frazzled and drained she seemed.

Gamilah called, too. She was working at the radio station where Mommy hosted a weekly talk show and she saw her often enough to notice how run-down she looked. I had my own reasons for being concerned. We had recently attended a Links luncheon and I noticed how tired she seemed. But when I asked, she insisted she was fine. After that, when I spoke to her on the telephone, Mommy sometimes sounded strange—lucid, but not quite herself.

One day I called out-of-the-blue to say I was coming by to see her. I had been having dinner with a friend of hers, Larry Dais, a vice president at Columbia University and a good friend of my mother's. We thought Mommy might appreciate a quick visit from the two of us. Arriving at the hotel where Mommy was staying temporarily, we knocked several times but got no answer.

We knocked again and finally she answered, but she still did not open the door. I thought her behavior was a little odd, but I wasn't alarmed because Mommy was very particular about the way she presented herself. I thought she didn't want to open the door, especially with Larry there, because she wasn't dressed.

Larry called through the door that he had some important papers he needed her to sign, which angered me. You selfish so-and-so, I thought. Something could be wrong with my mother and all you care about is getting your papers signed. Later I realized that Larry did not, in fact, have any such papers. He was just concerned about Mommy, too, and was trying to get her to open the door.

But his little subterfuge didn't work. Instead Mommy finally called through the door that she was fine but that she didn't want to be disturbed. "Listen, not tonight. I'm trying to get some rest."

We left, uneasy but not sure what else to do. Later that evening Mommy called to reassure me that she was fine. The following morning she asked me to come over and cook dinner for her. She asked for butternut squash, which I didn't know how to make. She told me and I followed her instructions and showed up at her door that night. It was January, clear but cold outside. I knocked on her door.

"Mommy? It's me."

"Okay, just a minute," she called, sounding like her regular self.

I waited, thinking she wanted to get herself dolled up before opening the door. A minute passed. Then two, then five, then fifteen, then I don't know how many. Every time I knocked, she called out, "Okay, sweetheart, just a minute."

"Mommy? Are you okay? Come to the door."

Finally, after what seemed like an hour or more, it dawned on me that something was not right. I ran to telephone the police. When they forced open the door, the first thing I saw was my mother's purse and her prized fur coat lying on the floor. My heart froze in my chest.

"Oh, my God," I said.

"Miss, maybe you better wait here," the police officer said.

But there was no way I was waiting outside when my mother needed me. She was lying on her bed, fully dressed, unable to move. Her eyes were open but she could not sit up or even speak. All she could do was look at me.

"Mommy, are you okay? Can you speak to me?" I called, but she could not respond.

It was the most frightening moment of my life. To see my mother, the woman who had guided my entire life and the lives of my sisters with her strong, steady hand, suddenly rendered helpless was like having the foundation on which I'd stood all my life knocked out from under me. We called an ambulance and rushed her to Westchester Medical Center.

At the emergency room they told me Mommy was severely dehydrated and physically exhausted. Her body, depleted to dangerous levels, had begun the process of shutting down and she needed urgent medical care. My voice trembling, I asked the doctor, "Will she be the same as she was before?"

"How was she before?" he asked. I could tell from his distracted attitude he didn't think much of this poor, crumbled African American woman he saw before him. He had no idea who she was or what she had done.

"She is strong and vibrant," I told him. "She's an educator with a Ph.D." But he just shrugged and said he could make no promises.

After a night in the intensive care unit, they moved my mother into a private room. I pulled two chairs near her bed and stretched myself out on them, wanting to be nearby when she woke up. By now I had been at the hospital for seventy-two hours and I was nearly delirious with fatigue. I wanted to go home, take a shower, change my clothes, and come back. But then Mommy opened her eyes and, semi-lucid, looked up at me. "Sweetheart, do you think you can stay with Mommy?"

"Of course, Mommy. You just rest."

And so I stayed. Attallah was in California and Qubilah was in Texas, but eventually Gamilah, Malikah, and Malaak arrived to relieve me.

Exhaustion had brought Mommy to the brink of death. But in the thirty-three days she remained in the hospital, she slowly came back to herself. As soon as she was alert enough, she wanted a clock and she wanted the newspaper read to her. Whatever she wanted, my sisters and I and my mother's close friends made sure she got.

I said everything I could think of to encourage her to get better. In the early days, when she was still struggling, I even told her a fib. My mother had a deep desire to see her daughters married, and she had introduced me to a certain local politician with that desire in mind. So I told her, "Mommy, you have to get better, because so-and-so and I are going to get married."

After Mommy was released from the hospital, her friend Mary Redd drove her home to my apartment where, over the course of a few months, I nursed her back to health. I saw a tender and vulnerable side of my mother. Over the next year we became closer than ever, not just mother and daughter but friends and confidantes.

Somewhere during this time Mommy's friend Ruth Dungie told me something Mommy had said to her while she was in the hospital. Ms. Dungie said Mommy looked up from her hospital bed with a smile and said, "I saw Malcolm."

Like all of us, Ms. Dungie was accustomed to my mother speaking of Daddy in the present tense. But this was different. Ms. Dungie told me Mommy said she saw my father and wanted to go with him, but Daddy said no.

"There is something more for you to do," he said. "You must go back."

You really get to see how God works in moments such as these. Had we lost Mommy at that time, in that way—helpless, broken, her beautiful mind fogged by dehydration—I don't think I could have handled it. I wasn't ready to let her go, and neither was the rest of her family, her daughters and her grandsons.

Daddy was right. We still needed her.

CHAPTER FOURTEEN

Reunited

our mother has been in a fire.

YI couldn't stop crying. The moment I heard those words on my answering machine, the tears began and refused to cease. I cried while I threw on my clothes, while I found my keys, and during the drive to Jacobi Hospital and the frantic dash to the emergency room. I was a river of tears that night, a wild, frightened, river of tears. It was as though my body was trying desperately to purge itself, to float away those words and the terrible truth they contained.

Your mother has been in a fire.

"Are you ready?" Someone was speaking to me. I forced myself to focus. It was a serious but kindly man who had introduced himself to me as Dr. Shef. He had his hand on the curtain that separated me from the most important person in my life.

I wanted to say *No! I'm not ready at all!* I stood on the other side of that curtain for what seemed an eternity, frightened, unable to move or think clearly, able only to pray. *Oh my God. Please help me. Please let Mommy be okay.* I was terrified of seeing her burned and helpless. I was terrified of that forever being the impression of my mother embedded in my mind. Surely that would be too much to bear.

But there was a larger part of me, perhaps the part inherited from my mother, that knew if I was on the other side of that curtain, Mommy would not hesitate to throw it aside. She would be there as she had always been for anyone who came into her life, especially her six daughters. And so I fought to get hold of myself. I had to be strong for her. I couldn't let her see me frightened and hysterical. She needed me now. I had to be in control.

"Yes, I am ready," I told Dr. Shef. I took a deep breath and we went in.

She was lying on a bed. She had been burned from the top of her beautiful head to the bottom of her feet, ninety-seven percent of her body. Eighty percent of the burns were third degree. Her flawless, honey brown skin was gone. I wanted to scream *Oh, Mommy . . . what happened to you, Mommy?!!* But I managed to strangle the sound in my throat.

"Hi, Mommy," I said in the most upbeat tone I could manage. "Ilyasah's here. You'll be okay."

I wanted to hold her in my arms and comfort her, but of course that was impossible. I couldn't even touch her or kiss her or look into her eyes, which were closed. The tears forced their way out and I felt myself falling apart. I had to get out of that room.

"I'll be right back, Mommy. We just need to take care of a few things, okay? I'll be right outside."

Once past the curtain, I had to grab hold of a chair to keep myself from falling to the floor. The image of my mother fighting her way through a fire, frightened and delirious with pain, was like a tidal wave that kept threatening to knock me down.

I was the one who chose the condo where the fire occurred; it was to be my home. Months before, my mother, in her never-ending drive to make sure all her daughters were provided for, had sent me to check out a handful of condos and co-op apartments. She didn't like the idea of my renting a place to live. She knew the importance of owning one's home, so she was going to help me buy a place.

I chose that particular condo in a lovely remodeled prewar building in Yonkers, right on the border of the village of Bronxville. The condo had high ceilings, a sunken living room, a fireplace, a spacious dining room, three bathrooms, lots of hallways and closets, and a maid's quarters just off the large, eat-in kitchen. It was a New York dream home, but it needed work. So I moved into a condo my mother had purchased for my sister Malaak in Mount Vernon. Malaak had left the condo to move somewhere else, and I moved in so my mother would not lose the money she had invested. My mother still had her home in Mount Vernon, but as renovations on the Yonkers condo neared completion, she began spending time there. And it was to this place that she often brought her first grandson, Malcolm.

Mommy had become Malcolm's legal guardian in 1995, after Qubilah, his mother, was charged in Minneapolis with conspiracy to murder Louis Farrakhan.

What I believe about that time is this: My sister was struggling and vulnerable. Like the rest of us, she wanted love and peace. Her son wanted a mother and father. They both just wanted to be a family. Then along comes this old acquaintance from my sister's days at the United Nations International School. He initiates contact; they spend long hours on the telephone, and gradually my sister falls in love. She believes this man loves her, too, is going to marry her. And then, somehow, the subject of Louis Farrakhan is raised. My sister, who has never focused on Farrakhan, never been a "black radical" or anything close to it, is suddenly caught up in this supposed conspiracy. And this man turns out to be an informant for the FBI.

I changed my major to biology in college, but I can still do the math.

My sister faced ninety years in prison and a $2 million fine. But shortly before her trial was to begin, a deal was struck: All charges would be dropped if Qubilah sought psychological treatment and alcohol-abuse treatment. She also had to temporarily relinquish her rights to Malcolm.

We all stepped in to care for Malcolm. Mommy was his legal guardian, but Malikah and I also shared custody of him. He thrived during those years with us in New York. He idolized Mommy Betty, as he called her. When he knew she was coming to my house to take him for an excursion, he would take a long shower then dress himself meticulously, buttoning his shirt all the way to the neck and tucking in the bottom. He would excitedly gather his books and papers and magazines to take along with him to show off his grades or some article he'd read, prompting a stimulating conversation between the two of them. Mommy Betty treated Malcolm as if he were a responsible, mature, and well-rounded young man and he believed that he was.

Malcolm loved Mommy Betty and she loved him. We all did (and still do). During those years in New York he was our pride and joy: disciplined, respectful, compassionate. He had a heart as big as the sky. Once, in a report, he wrote, "If there was one thing in the whole wide world that I could do, I'd help the homeless people. I'd feed them and give them clothes because they are hungry and their clothes are ripped."

He and I shared a special bond. I wanted him to feel that he could talk to me about anything. I tried to teach him the same important lessons my mother had taught me and some she had not because life was different in the 1990s. When Malcolm was about six years old I would say, "Okay, Malcolm, what do you say if someone tries to offer you drugs?"

"Beat it! Scram, you loser!" he'd respond, utterly serious. It made me smile inside.

But as much as we loved Malcolm, as hard as we tried, we could never be his mother. After Qubilah successfully completed counseling and substance-abuse treatment, Malcolm went to Texas to be with her. He was so happy. At his new school he made the honor roll and played on the basketball team. During one game, he told me, he made a great shot and the crowd went wild. They screamed *Malcolm, Malcolm, Malcolm can . . . If he can't do it, nobody can.*

"And you know what my mom did," he asked me.

"No, Malcolm. What did she do?"

"Auntie, she came down on the court and said, 'Come here, baby, and give Mommy a kiss!' "

By now I couldn't stop laughing, but I managed to ask Malcolm what he did.

"I ignored her!" he said, sounding like a typical adolescent. But I knew he was thrilled to have his mother demonstrate her love and pride so publicly.

But then things began to change. About a month later, Malcolm told me on the telephone he understood why Mommy Betty didn't want him with his mom. He said he thought it would be best for him to come back to New York. Then, later, he felt his mom needed him and he wanted to stay. But Qubilah was struggling again. She and her new husband had separated. Malcolm was missing school and acting out. After about three months, Mommy told Qubilah to send Malcolm back to us.

When I saw Malcolm this time, I knew something was wrong. He had changed. Gone was the sweet, innocent, nerdy boy I had known. Some days were good, others weren't. About three weeks before the fire, my mother called me in Florida where I was vacationing. Malcolm had disappeared. Shortly after my mother's call, I was paged by security at my housing complex. They said a neighbor found a boy who claimed to be my nephew. It was Malcolm. I telephoned Malikah to ask her to go get him, then called Mommy to tell her everything was all right. But a few days later, he left again. My mother had taken him bowling and he just wandered off.

Mommy came to my office to tell me. "Ilyasah, what do I do?" she asked. I was so busy with work, but at her words I stopped what I was doing, shocked at the helpless tone of her voice. Was this my mother, asking for help?

I got on the phone to officials at LaGuardia Airport, knowing Malcolm wanted to go back to Texas and be under his mother's guardianship. And sure enough, it turned out a handsome young boy was trying to buy a ticket to Texas. I called Qubilah to alert her, then got my mother in the car and drove to the airport. Once there, my mother tried to get out of the car but I told her to stay put; I would handle this. It turned out Malcolm had already left, but I was paged by Qubilah, who told me Malcolm had called her to say he was on his way home. She made it clear she could not handle him.

We alerted officials at Port Authority, and later police there called to say they had Malcolm in custody and would hold him until we arrived. Again my mother tried to come inside with me and again I told her to stay in the car. Inside I found my nephew and tried to explain what he was doing to Mommy Betty and to himself by running away. He was apologetic and ashamed and we all went home, praying a corner had been turned, that we had finally gotten through to him.

But is there a way to get through to a twelve-year-old child? Is there a way to make him truly understand why he cannot be with the most important person in his life? Maybe we could have tried harder to explain why his mother was not able to provide the attention he needed right then. Maybe we could have done a better job of making him understand that being with us was the best place for him at that time. I know we all did the best we could. I think of my elementary school teacher Mr. Schneider intoning, *You will regret*. And I try not to regret.

It was a very small fire at first, set in the hallway just outside of Malcolm's room. Later, devastated and full of remorse, Malcolm told me he did not intend to hurt anyone, least of all Mommy Betty. He thought she would telephone for help and the fire would be easily extinguished and everyone would see how much he needed to be back in Texas with his mom.

But my mother was self-reliant and always put everyone else's needs before her own. She always thought about her family first. I know she must have awakened, seen the smoke and fire, and believed the entire apartment was ablaze. I'm certain her first and fiercest thoughts were of Malcolm. He had run to a neighbor's and said he needed to call the fire department because his grandmother's house was on fire, but Mommy didn't know that. She probably thought Malcolm was still in his room. And if her grandson was in that fire, she was not going to wait. She was going to get him out herself.

She must have started down the long hallway that connected the master bedroom where she slept with Malcolm's room and then the living room. But she didn't make it. Her neighbor Beth told police she heard a loud thump and found my mother lying on the floor and the apartment full of smoke. She immediately called for help. Beth said my mother had the strength to say a few words before she lost consciousness.

"My grandson," she said. "I need some water . . . a doctor . . . my bag."

The doctors warned me Mommy was unconscious. In fact, they said she was, essentially, gone.

"It's only a matter of time," the doctors said. "She will not make it."

They kept saying something about papers, something about needing to accept and to sign, but my head was swimming and their words seemed to be coming to me from high above, as though I had been plunged to the bottom of a deep, deep well. *Gone? Papers? This can't be happening, not to Mommy.* I kept praying, talking to God. *Please, Lord. She can't be gone.*

I never felt so alone in all my life. Was this how Mommy felt on that day in the Audubon?

Someone said, "We're moving your mother to the burn unit to bandage her. Have you called your family? Are they on their way? They need to hurry." And then those words again:

"She will not make it."

I found a telephone and started dialing. I tried to reach Percy Sutton and one of Mommy's closest friends in New York, Mary Redd. I called Terrie Williams, and then I called my friend Kathy in Connecticut and asked her to come. Then I braced myself for what I knew would be the hardest calls: the ones to my sisters.

I called Qubilah, in Texas. She burst into tears and told me to pray; she would catch the next plane out.

By then it was almost three o'clock in the morning. I tried calling Attallah in California, but she wasn't home so I left a jumbled, frightened message on her answering machine. Every time I dialed Malikah's number I'd hang up. Malikah was sensitive and vulnerable and she, too, was very close to Mommy. I didn't know how she would handle such incomprehensible news. But I had to tell her and so finally I let the phone ring.

"Malikah." I spoke soothingly, slowly, trying to give her the news as gently as I could. "Mommy's been in a fire."

"What?" The confusion and terror in her voice made me wince.

"It's not good," I said.

She started to cry. I told her to find my nephew Malcolm, but she said the police had already called and told her they had him at Mount Vernon Hospital, smelling of gasoline. What this information indicated was too much for me to think about right then, so I pushed it from my mind.

"Go get him and bring him here," I told Malikah, not realizing that Malcolm was in police custody.

I decided to wait awhile before calling Gamilah because I knew such terrible news would be too much for her to handle in the middle of the night. I didn't know how or where to reach Malaak, so I called her friend Peekoo in the city and left a message that it was urgent she contact me as soon as possible.

Mary Redd arrived at the hospital, followed shortly by Kathy, who had driven over from Westport. Malikah showed up, but without Malcolm. She had gone to the police station, found Malcolm in custody, smelled the gasoline on his clothes, and erupted with anger and with fear. "What did you do to my mother, Malcolm?" she screamed at him.

The police had taken Malcolm to Mount Vernon Hospital for an evaluation. Early Sunday morning, almost six hours after the tragedy, I left Mommy's bedside briefly to go check on my nephew. I was accompanied by Percy Sutton and Larry Dais.

We found Malcolm lying on his side on a slender white cot, accompanied by several police detectives. He had on a hospital gown and his beautiful, slender brown feet were bare; the police told us his clothes contained gasoline.

I was nearly delirious with shock and fatigue. I looked at Malcolm and thought, *My poor baby. His life is over. He'll spend the rest of his life in jail, agonizing over what he did.* And then, in the next moment, I looked at his bare feet and thought, *I have to buy him a pair of sneakers.*

He didn't want to talk and, like my sister, my fear made me furious. "You better tell me what happened, Malcolm," I said, raising my voice. "Mommy Betty is lying in a hospital burned from head to toe!"

He was stunned. His eyes filled with tears and fear and grief, but I don't think he fully understood. Anyone who knew Mommy could never believe her predicament unless he saw her with his own eyes. Malcolm was mature for his age, insightful and logical, but at that moment he looked like the child he was. He looked like a frightened child who didn't know what he had done and didn't know what was going to happen to him. He only knew Mommy Betty wasn't there to fix whatever had gone so terribly wrong. It broke my heart.

If Mommy ever knew it was Malcolm who set the fire, she didn't hear it from me. She did learn that Malcolm was okay and I know that information set her mind at ease, thank God.

After leaving Mount Vernon Hospital, Mr. Sutton, Mr. Dais, and I went to the Yonkers apartment. By now reporters were swarming all over the place, but the police kept them back from the apartment itself. As we walked up six flights of stairs—the elevator was taped off—I saw Beth. She hugged me and told me how she had found my mother. I was grateful to her, but hearing the story was so painful I could barely stand it.

The press had also made its way to Jacobi Hospital in full force by the time we returned. We climbed from our car and were immediately swarmed by cameramen and photographers and reporters pushing microphones into our faces, but I was so consumed with my mother's condition I scarcely noticed them. My friend Kathy appeared and fought the press off as if she were fighting off a pack of wild dogs. She escorted me to the hospital library, the place that would become our home away from home for the time Mommy had left upon this earth.

At this point, Malikah and I were the only daughters at the hospital. We were waiting in the library, too stunned, panicked, and heartbroken to do anything but pray. Then Ms. Deitrich, a nurse, arrived with heart-stopping news.

"Your mother is conscious," she said. "Your mother wants to see you."

Malikah and I immediately jumped up. *Mommy was conscious!* We started toward the burn unit but the nurse stopped us. "No," she said, gently but firmly. "She wants to see you," the nurse said, pointing to me.

The nurse told us Mommy had awakened and become fidgety and agitated, as if she were trying to speak. She could not open her eyes or her mouth, so the nurse gave her a clipboard, wrapped a pen with gauze and tape, and gently slipped it between her fingers. Slowly, painfully, Mommy managed to communicate to the nurse what she wanted.

My heart was pounding and my pulse raced. All I could think was *She's alive! She's alive!* I had so feared that she would never regain consciousness. The nurse handed me the precautionary sterile garb I had to wear—shoe covers, gown, cap, gloves, and mask—and I threw them on, trembling with grief and hope and joy. The doctors had told me, had insisted, that Mommy was not going to make it; they had assured me she was all but gone. And then, suddenly, there she was: alive and asking for me. I was getting the chance to see her again. To talk to her.

As I entered her room, I saw that they had now bandaged her from head to toe.

"Hi, Mommy!" I said with the excitement of a child. I knew she could hear me now and I didn't want to let her know how bad it was.

"Hi, precious! Hi, angel. Yasah's here, baby." I fought to hold back my tears but failed. I knew Mommy could not see me, but I didn't want her to sense my pain.

She could barely move but she was trying desperately to write, to clutch that pen and move it across that pad of paper nearby. It was unbearable to watch.

"Mommy," I said. "Oh, Mommy. You don't have to write anything to me. Whatever is in your heart is in my heart. Just relax, baby. You don't have to worry about anything. You need to conserve your energy, okay? I'll take care of you, Mommy."

Slowly Mommy lifted her bandaged arms. As gently as possible I moved beneath the arms and received her hug, my heart strained by pain and joy. This moment above all others, this last physical contact with my mother, is etched forever in my memory and forever in my heart.

"Oh, thank you, Mommy," I said, tears washing my face. "I love you. You've been the best mom. Now you need to conserve your energy and relax, Mommy. Okay? Yasah'll take care of you. I'm gonna do everything I know you want me to do. Just relax, honey. I love you so much, my sweetheart. I love you so much. Just relax."

I kept talking to her, fighting to be as comforting and as strong as possible. When I looked up I saw Malikah at the door and my heart went out to her. It was painful for her to see me with Mommy, but I know she knows that Mommy loved each of her daughters in a very special and unique way. We were all her babies, her special girls. We all have invaluable memories and precious firsthand lessons learned at Mommy's side that no one can ever take away. And as daughters and sisters, we all share a special, priceless bond. We are family.

Despite the doctor's predictions, Mommy not only lived through the night, but defied modern medicine and kept living for twenty-two days. I believe she stayed alive for us, to give us time to prepare for life without her. The doctors said only a fraction of people who suffer the degree of burns Mommy suffered survive. But we knew if anyone could beat those odds, it would be our mother.

By Tuesday all of my sisters had arrived and we sat down for a heartrending family discussion. As always, Mr. Sutton was by our side. The doctors were gently advising us to disconnect Mommy's life support. I am ashamed to admit it now, but after seeing her that first day as no one else had, I was willing to do it. I couldn't bear to see her suffer that way one minute more. I wanted to let her go in peace and Mary Redd agreed with me.

But Malikah was adamantly, vehemently opposed to disconnecting the life support. She wanted to do as much as possible for as long as possible. One by one, we all came to agree with Malikah because none of us wanted to lose Mommy; the idea was almost unbearable. We decided to leave Mommy on life support and prayed for a miracle.

At first, Gamilah could not understand how I could spend so much time in that room, talking and singing to Mommy as if

229

nothing had happened to her. To see a loved one suffer is one of the hardest things for anyone to bear. But it was especially painful for my sisters and me to see Mommy suffer in the way she did. Our mother had always taken such pride in her flawless brown skin. It was one of the things Daddy loved about her, and her pride in her color at a time when too many African Americans saw only shame in physical connection to Africa is one of the characteristics that made my mother so unique. To see that skin so ravaged and burned was devastating. The only way I could cope looking at her was to think about what Kedar had said to me many years ago: "We are simply spirits in a shell. The body is merely a covering, a casement for the soul."

I knew that inside her casing, Mommy was still as beautiful and as strong as ever. Her soul could not be touched, and so I focused on that soul, on the mommy I knew was inside. I loved her so much. And I knew by her hug that she was not only telling me that she loved me, she was telling me to carry on.

I never got to hug her again. From then on, she would communicate with us by pulling her legs together or by slowly moving her left foot to let us know she was alert and could hear us. There were so many international and national dignitaries, so many educators, celebrities, theologians, family members, friends, strangers, so many well wishers, young and old and of every ethnic origin who came to pay their respects. The most memorable was certainly the telephone call that came from President Bill Clinton. My sisters and I were deeply moved by his expressions of concern and support. Mommy admired both Bill and Hillary Clinton; she would have been pleased to know they were thinking of her.

Former mayor Ed Koch, Mayor Rudolph Giuliani, Governor

George Pataki, and many, many others also called and visited. Dr. Maya Angelou, one of Mommy's great friends, came and stayed with us. Bernice King came with her mother, Coretta, and brought God's healing balm through prayer. Restaurant owners and staff sent delicious food to sustain us through the ordeal. So many people from my past—friends, teachers, professors—extended their love and support during this time, and I am forever grateful. My sisters and I were overwhelmed with the most beautiful flowers, gifts, cards, letters, and prayers from all over the world. We all felt comforted in knowing Mommy had touched so many people by just being herself.

The hospital staff was likewise wonderful. All the nurses, doctors, aides, and orderlies embraced us like family and supported us through the entire ordeal. Even an unknown police officer reached out. One night we had a big scare. Mommy seemed to be fading and one of her doctors who lived on Long Island was paged. As he raced back to the hospital, he was pulled over for speeding by a police officer. When he explained whose doctor he was and why he was moving so fast, the police officer provided an escort all the way to the hospital. Other police officers volunteered to provide security for us.

Sitting with Mommy one day I said, "Mommy, there are people who jump up and down, and say, 'Look at me! Look at what I've done!' But by just being yourself, you have drawn people to you. Your efforts and humane deeds are being recognized all over the world. And I'm so proud to be your daughter. You've set the best example for us."

I know that whatever my mother did, she did from the heart. I believe that is God's most gracious blessing.

During those twenty-two days we provided a lot of quiet activity for Mommy. I updated her on the news and reported the results of the basketball finals and of Mike Tyson's latest fight. She seemed to understand and had reached out to Mike Tyson.

All of Mommy's daughters were there for her, doing what they could. Once, when things seemed to be going downhill, Malikah stayed up all night juicing garlic. I'll never forget that night. We were all so scared, my sisters and I. We didn't know what was going to happen and we didn't know if we could handle it. When Malikah finished the garlic juice, the nurses put it into Mommy's IV and, for a while, she seemed to rally. We were so full of hope. We gathered around Malikah, crying and hugging. We were like "All hail, Malikah!" God bless her because heaven knows she tried to keep her mother alive. We all tried so hard. But God had other plans.

On the day before Mommy left us, I stood by her bed. She was rapidly deteriorating and no longer conscious; my sisters and I could see her leaving before our eyes. In our grief and pain we began to feud, all the fears and wounds of childhood churned up by the emotion of the moment. I felt the grief that had built inside me since that phone call, the grief I had tried so hard to hide behind a wall of strength for Mommy's sake, come bursting through like an avalanche. I wept and cried and pleaded like a child:

"Please don't go, Mommy! Please don't go. I need you!"

It was pure selfishness, but I could not help myself. I knew she had only held on for her daughters and her grandchildren. I knew that, for the first time in her life, she would finally have peace. I knew she would be with the Creator and be with her husband again. I knew all that from the very first moment of the accident and still my heart broke to lose her. To see her go.

The following day, June 23, 1997, my mother made her transition. It was thirty-two years and four months after my father made his.

I wasn't there when she took her last breath. I was with Mr. Sutton at the bank going through her safe-deposit box looking for her will. By the time I got back to the hospital, she was gone.

After comforting one another, my sisters and I performed a J'naaza, a Muslim burial ritual. Sister Aisha al-Adawiya from our mosque assisted us. She had been there with us from the early hours of the tragedy, praying over Mommy and humming recitations from the Qur'an with a steadiness that came to seem like music, like a fragrant offering to my mother and a balm to my sisters and me. Her daughter, Suhailah, also came from Atlanta to be with us, despite the fact that we had not seen her in years.

Following Sister Aisha's instructions, we gently dabbed Mommy with holy water, salts, and oils. We then wrapped her in white linen and silks, just as Daddy had been wrapped and prepared. When we finished, we tied a crisp, beautiful bow beneath Mommy's breasts, just as our Egyptian and Ethiopian ancestors had done thousands and thousands of years before. Mommy wanted to be buried on top of our father, and we planned to honor her request.

That time of preparing Mommy's body was painful, but also healing for my sisters and me. It was like a sonnet we wrote to her, expressing our love and appreciation for all she had been to each of us. In the actions of my five proud, strong-willed and yet vulnerable sisters that day, I saw their gentility, their love. I saw their respect and idolization for their mother, for Mommy. I saw myself.

When we finished the burial ritual Mommy looked like the beautiful queen she always was to all of us. A beautiful queen dressed all in white who, having raised her daughters and sent them into the world to carry on the fight, was now going to greet her king.

There was a time in my life when I believed that if something happened to my mother, I would crumble, would be completely and utterly lost. And not only would I be lost, but all the projects Mommy undertook, all the people she helped and her continuing effort to advance my father's legacy—all this would also fall by the wayside, because who could possibly step into Mommy's shoes?

But if my mother taught me anything, it was perseverance. Even in the face of adversity. Even in the face of pain.

I remember once asking her how she found the strength to carry on after her husband was taken. She said, "You know, sweetheart, life goes on. You can sit back and cry, but in the meantime life goes on. Society has so many ills and someone has to fix them. We each have a purpose and a mission in life, and our mission is not to sit back and feel sorry for ourselves."

My mother's mission was to leave the world a better place than she found it and she far surpassed that personal goal. Now it is our turn to carry on—my sisters, Mommy's friends, the hundreds upon hundreds of young people she touched all over the world. We no longer have Betty Shabazz or Malcolm X physically, but we can all carry their spirits in our hearts.

None of us has to live a life of bitterness. None of us has to live a life of despair. Like my mother and father, we all have the capacity to make the world a better place if we only stand up and demand that it be so. If we only challenge injustice and oppression in every shape and form.

A male student attending Medgar Evers College told me a story of my mother that I love. He said he was hanging in the hallway one day with some of the boys when Dr. Shabazz approached. They all became flustered; they didn't know what to say to her. But the student told me Mommy was warm and loving, and she told him something he will remember for a lifetime. She said, "You come from great ancestors. Act like it."

Life is not a destination; it is a journey. Faith makes everything possible. In order to succeed in life, we must first believe that we can.

About the Author

ILYASAH SHABAZZ holds a master of science degree in education and human resource development from Fordham University. She is the Director of Public Affairs and Special Events for the city of Mount Vernon, New York.